JAMES HOGG

Mador of the Moor

THE STIRLING / SOUTH CAROLINA RESEARCH EDITION OF

THE COLLECTED WORKS OF JAMES HOGG

GENERAL EDITORS – DOUGLAS S. MACK AND GILLIAN HUGHES

THE STIRLING / SOUTH CAROLINA RESEARCH EDITION OF
THE COLLECTED WORKS OF JAMES HOGG
GENERAL EDITORS – DOUGLAS S. MACK AND GILLIAN HUGHES

Volumes are numbered in the order of their publication in
the Stirling / South Carolina Research Edition

JAMES HOGG

Mador of the Moor

Edited by
James E. Barcus

With an Essay on Hogg's Literary Friendships
by Janette Currie
and an Appendix on the Popular Context
by Suzanne Gilbert

EDINBURGH UNIVERSITY PRESS

2005

© Edinburgh University Press, 2005

Edinburgh University Press
22 George Square
Edinburgh
EH8 9LF

Typeset at the University of Stirling
Printed by MPG Books Ltd, Bodmin

ISBN 0 7486 1807 4

A CIP record for this book is available from the British Library

The Stirling / South Carolina Research Edition of

The Collected Works of James Hogg

The Aims of the Edition

James Hogg lived from 1770 till 1835. He was regarded by his con-
temporaries as one of the leading writers of the day, but the nature
of his fame was influenced by the fact that, as a young man, he had
been a self-educated shepherd. The second edition (1813) of his
poem *The Queen's Wake* contains an 'Advertisement' which begins as
follows.

> THE *Publisher having been favoured with letters from gentlemen in vari-
> ous parts of the United Kingdom respecting the Author of the* QUEEN'S

WAKE, *and most of them expressing doubts of his being a Scotch Shepherd; he takes this opportunity of assuring the Public, that* THE QUEEN'S WAKE *is really and truly the production of* JAMES HOGG, *a* common shepherd, *bred among the mountains of Ettrick Forest, who went to service when only seven years of age; and since that period has never received any education whatever.*

The view of Hogg taken by his contemporaries is also reflected in the various early reviews of *The Private Memoirs and Confessions of a Justified Sinner*, which appeared anonymously in 1824. As Gillian Hughes has shown in the *Newsletter of the James Hogg Society* no. 1, many of these reviews identify Hogg as the author, and see the novel as presenting 'an incongruous mixture of the strongest powers with the strongest absurdities'. The Scotch Shepherd was regarded as a man of powerful and original talent, but it was felt that his lack of education caused his work to be marred by frequent failures in discretion, in expression, and in knowledge of the world. Worst of all was Hogg's lack of what was called 'delicacy', a failing which caused him to deal in his writings with subjects (such as prostitution) which were felt to be unsuitable for mention in polite literature. Hogg was regarded as a man of undoubted genius, but his genius was felt to be seriously flawed.

A posthumous collected edition of Hogg was published in the late 1830s. As was perhaps natural in the circumstances, the publishers (Blackie & Son of Glasgow) took pains to smooth away what they took to be the rough edges of Hogg's writing, and to remove his numerous 'indelicacies'. This process was taken even further in the 1860s, when the Rev. Thomas Thomson prepared a revised edition of Hogg's *Works* for publication by Blackie. These Blackie editions present a bland and lifeless version of Hogg's writings. It was in this version that Hogg was read by the Victorians. Unsurprisingly, he came to be regarded as a minor figure, of no great importance or interest.

The second half of the twentieth century saw a substantial revival of Hogg's reputation; and he is now generally considered to be one of Scotland's major writers. This new reputation is based on a few works which have been republished in editions based on his original texts. Nevertheless, a number of Hogg's major works remain out of print. Indeed, some have been out of print for more than a century and a half, while others, still less fortunate, have never been published at all in their original, unbowdlerised condition.

Hogg is thus a major writer whose true stature was not recognised in his own lifetime because his social origins led to his being smothered in genteel condescension; and whose true stature has not been recognised since, because of a lack of adequate editions. The poet Douglas Dunn wrote of Hogg in the *Glasgow Herald* in September 1988: 'I can't help but think that in almost any other country of Europe a complete, modern edition of a comparable author would have been available long ago'. The Stirling / South Carolina Edition of James Hogg seeks to fill the gap identified by Douglas Dunn. When completed the edition will run to thirty-four volumes; and it will cover Hogg's prose, his poetry, and his plays.

General Editors' Acknowledgements

We are grateful for the support of the University of Stirling and the University of South Carolina, and for assistance from the Association for Scottish Literary Studies and the James Hogg Society. We also record with gratitude the fact that the substantial contributions of Dr Gillian Hughes and Dr Janette Currie to the present volume (see Volume Editor's Acknowledgements) were made possible by a major research grant awarded by the United Kingdom's Arts and Humanities Research Board to the Stirling / South Carolina Edition of James Hogg. Dr Suzanne Gilbert was General Editor for the present volume.

Volume Editor's Acknowledgements

Acknowledging intellectual and emotional and financial support on a project completed over several years inevitably will lead to omissions and oversights. For these, I apologise in advance. However, among those who deserve special notice are Professor Douglas Mack and Dr Suzanne Gilbert of Stirling University. From my earliest correspondence with Professor Mack to the final suggestions from Dr Gilbert, these scholars helped to shape the intellectual structure of the final manuscript, to point out significant and relevant historical details, and to monitor accuracy. I cannot acknowledge adequately the degree to which I am in their debt. Particular thanks are also due to Dr J. H. Alexander for many detailed and valuable suggestions, and to Dr Gillian Hughes of Stirling University, who very kindly gave me invaluable access to materials to be included in her Stirling / South Carolina edition of Hogg's *Letters*. Dr Hughes's research for her edition of Hogg's *Letters* has been funded by the United Kingdom's Arts and Humanities Research Board. The AHRB-funded assistance of Dr Janette Currie of Stirling University on *Mador of the Moor* has also been of great value, not least for her contribution to the preparation of the Glossary. And this volume owes a considerable debt to Wilma Mack's careful attention to detail, not least in proofreading.

Financial and other support for this edition of James Hogg's *Mador of the Moor* has come from a variety of sources, including the University of Stirling, the University of South Carolina, and other societies and trusts. In addition, Baylor University in Waco, Texas, provided me with a ten-month sabbatical to complete the project and a travel grant, permitting me to spend essential time in Scotland and England. I have no adequate means to express my appreciation to the Administration of Baylor University for this support. However, Dr Herbert H. Reynolds, now president-emeritus of Baylor University, should also be recognised for the encouragement and inspiration he gave to me, and to other university scholars, during his tenure as president. Baylor University also provided financial support for two student assistants, Brian Newsome and Stan Coppinger, who helped to check references, proofread the manuscript, and prepare it for publication. The seriousness with which they carried out these tasks speaks clearly to their potential as scholars.

Scholars without librarians are fish without water. Numerous librarians have played significant roles in bringing the project to conclusion. The staff in the interlibrary loan office of the Baylor University libraries searched diligently for necessary editions and supporting materials, and the reference librarians laboured assiduously to meet my requests. All were more than accommodating. And the librarians and staff of the Stirling University Library provided this visiting scholar with every courtesy and assistance one might expect. I wish to recognise particularly Susan R. Swain in the Special Collections of the Mary Couts Burnett Library, Texas Christian University, Fort Worth, Texas, for providing access to the very rare 1816 American edition of *Mador of the Moor*. I am also grateful to the John Murray Archive and to the Trustees of the National Library of Scotland for permission to quote from manuscript and other material in their collections.

Finally, I dedicate this volume to three of my best teachers: my children Heidi, Jeff, and Hans.

James E. Barcus
Baylor University

Contents

KINCRAIGY.
ON THE TAY.

Illustration by D.O. Hill of the Tay at Kincraigy and Kinnaird.
From *The Works of The Ettrick Shepherd*, ed. by T. Thomson (1878)

Introduction

Origin and Reception

According to Hogg, credit for his beginning to write *Mador of the Moor* must be given to Mrs Chalmers [Eliza] Izett. In 1814, on one of his annual summer tours of the Highlands, Hogg was suffering with a severe cold, and his friends the Izetts arranged for him to remain for 'two or three weeks' at their Highland home, Kinnaird House, which is situated midway between Dunkeld and Pitlochry, and which overlooks the River Tay. Believing that Hogg should redeem his time, Mrs Izett gave him the use of a study complete with books and writing materials. In a scene reminiscent of Lady Austen setting William Cowper to work on the poem known as *The Task*, Mrs Izett insists that Hogg write. Here is Hogg's account:

> "Now," said she, "I do not wish you to curtail your fishing hours, since you seem to delight so much in it, but whenever you have a spare hour, either evening or morning, you can retire to this place, either to read or write, as the humour suits you."—"Since you will set me down to write," said I, "you must choose a subject for me, for I have nothing in hand, and have thought of nothing."—"How can you be at loss for a subject," returned she, "and that majestic river [the Tay] rolling beneath your eyes?"—"Well," said I, "though I consider myself exquisite at descriptions of nature, and mountain-scenery in particular, yet I am afraid that a poem wholly descriptive will prove dull and heavy."—"You may make it the shorter," said she; "only write something to prevent your mind from rusting."[1]

Hogg adds that he 'determined immediately to write a poem descriptive of the river Tay' and that after two hours spent considering what verse form to use, he settled on the Spenserian stanza. Although there is no external evidence to confirm Hogg's account, internal evidence supports two of his contentions. First, as the editorial matter of this edition documents, Hogg's allusions and descriptions are precise to the minute detail. This poem also confirms Hogg's assessment of his ability to describe nature, especially mountain scenery. From Kincraigy to Cairn-Gorm, from the Tilt to Dunfermline, from Braemar to Stirling, Hogg knows his geography, his place-names, and his history. And he recreates his visual experiences in moving verbal passages.

We do not know how much time Hogg devoted to writing *Mador of the Moor*. In his 'Memoir' he says it was composed in 1814, but, as Gillian Hughes has demonstrated,[2] his account in the 'Memoir' of the genesis of *Mador* needs to be questioned, supplemented, and perhaps corrected by reference to other sources. For example, Hogg's memoir date of 1814 does not agree with his announcement in a letter to Alexander Bald dated 14 November 1813.

> Since my return from the Highlands I have been very busy with a new poem which already extends to 1100 lines and no appearance of any close. It is in the stanza of Spencer and much of it descriptive of Highland scenery and manners you will perhaps live to see the Highlanders described differently from Mrs. Grant. The approbation it has recieved has rather astonished me at myself, and I am at a loss how to proceed, or whether to proceed at all or not.[3]

This letter gives no credit to Elizabeth Izett and indicates that *Mador* was begun in 1813, not 1814. Moreover, in a letter to Archibald Constable, dated 1 February 1814, Hogg claims, with apparent reference to *Mador*, 'excepting a few notes &c. I have finished a poem of 2200 lines or thereabout'. Writing in retrospect in the 'Memoir', he may have confused an 1813 visit to the Highlands with an 1814 journey.

There is no reason not to credit the influence of Elizabeth Izett, in spite of the obvious allusion to Cowper and Lady Austen, in light of Mrs Izett's various literary interests. Although biographical details are slight, recent research shows that she married Chalmers Izett about April 1797 at Dowally, Perthshire. Post Office Directories indicate that from about 1804 till around the beginning of 1810 the Izetts lived at 6 St John Street in the Canongate district of Edinburgh, where their neighbours included the novelist Mary Brunton and her husband Alexander, who lived at 3 St John Street. According to the biographical preface to Brunton's posthumously published *Emmeline* (Edinburgh, 1819), Brunton and Elizabeth were intimate friends, and the preface gives extracts, primarily on religious subjects, from letters the two exchanged. More than a decade later, Mrs Izett became concerned about the threatened sale and dispersion of the library of the church historian John Lee, and corresponded with him on the subject. Lee (1779–1859) became minister of the

Canongate Church in 1821, and was Principal of Edinburgh University from 1840 till 1859. Clearly, Elizabeth Izett played an active role in some literary circles. For further discussion of Hogg's relationship with her, and with John Grieve (to whom *Mador of the Moor* is dedicated), see the relevant entries in Gillian Hughes's 'Notes on Correspondents' in Hogg's *Collected Letters Volume 1 1800–1819* (S/ SC, 2004), as well as Janette Currie's essay which follows this Introduction.

In spite of Hogg's assertion to Constable that the poem was finished by 1 February 1814, he tells Elizabeth Izett in a letter of 11 February 1814 that the poem is not yet completed:

> I have not yet finished my poem it has so interested me I cannot get quit of it—it now amounts to 2300 lines and is divided into six cantos I am positively within a few lines of the end now

As published, *Mador* has only five cantos: in the 'Memoir' (p. 35) Hogg writes 'I left out to the extent of one whole book of the descriptive part'. In the letter just quoted he adds,

> Some ladies of high distinguishment in letters [Is he referring to Elizabeth Izett?] have objected strongly to the title *Mador of the Moor* but Grieve who delights in such a dark mysterious title will by no means yeild to the giving it up I have been thinking of calling it *The Maiden of Tay* pray think upon it—

Between 1814 and the appearance of the poem in 1816, Hogg continues to work on and essentially advertise the work. On 3 June 1814, he writes to Byron:

> I have finished another poem in the Spenserian stanza six months ago but I am terrified for publishing too much and in spite both of vanity and necessity I have prevailed upon myself to let it lie over for some time—

To John Murray, he writes on 21 January 1815,

> I have another poem ready whenever you like to put it to the press it is not nearly equal to the Pilgrims, but more congenial to human feelings and all in one kind of verse.

And again to Murray on 13 March 1815,

> I should like much to have something going on this spring as I will be engaged all the summer in the country; and I shall either publish *Mador of the Moor* a poem rather longer than the

Pilgrims or *The Thistle and the Rose* the work of which we were talking.

It is clear that Hogg corrected proofs of *Mador of the Moor* (though how diligently it is impossible to say). On 17 March [1816] he writes to Eliza Izett:

It is likely that I will tarry for some time here [Edinburgh] as my poem of Mador is gone to the press and about the beginning of May you may expect such a description of your own scenery as you have not yet seen in verse.[5]

On 8 April 1816 Hogg tells John Whitfeld that he will remain in Edinburgh about a month for he is 'publishing a new Poem which will appear in a week or two'. And on 11 April he reports to Blackwood that

The last sheets are now in my hands but I have no notes ready nor do I care much about them [...]. Query is the book large enough or would it be the better for a sheet of notes or short poems?

Hogg here refers to Scott's practice of embellishing his long narrative poems with extensive explanatory and background notes—a practice Hogg himself had followed in *The Queen's Wake* (1813).

According to the 'Memoir' (p. 35), James Park of Greenock read *Mador*, *Pilgrims of the Sun*, and other poems in manuscript. Park persuaded Hogg to give priority to *Pilgrims of the Sun*, a decision that Hogg came to regret because 'as an entire poem by itself, it bears an impress of extravagance, and affords no relief from the story of a visionary existence' ('Memoir', p. 36). William Blackwood did, in fact, publish *Pilgrims of the Sun* in December 1814 and then *Mador of the Moor* in April 1816. In both cases the poems were published by Blackwood in Edinburgh in partnership with John Murray in London. Blackwood informs Murray on 11 March 1816 that Hogg

is however determined to print just now, and is going to put to press Mador of the Moor, a Poem which he has had ready for some time. I read it nearly twelve months ago, and liked it pretty well [...]. He proposes only to print 500 or 750.[4]

Unfortunately, records of print runs are sporadic and the exact print run is not known. The precise date of publication in Edinburgh was 22 April, as Gillian Hughes has established. On that day it was advertised as 'This day is published' in the *Edinburgh Evening Courant* of 22 April 1816, and it is listed among the 'New Works Published in Edinburgh' in the *Scots Magazine*, 78 (April 1816), 292.[6] Initial sales may not have lived up to Blackwood's expectations, for he tells Murray on 27 April 1816 that 'Hogg's Poem is not doing much, but there are a number of beautiful passages which will make it sell. You will do what you can for it'. However by 6/7 June 1816, Blackwood, writing to Murray, is relieved to hear that the sales are improving. 'I am happy to hear Mador has been doing so well. The Shepherd will be quite elated when he hears of it—he is at present in the Highlands exploring the wild scenery of Argyleshire'.[7] Since sales records are incomplete, definitive figures are not available for *Mador*, but one Murray catalogue indicates that he still had copies on hand in May 1817.[8]

During Hogg's lifetime, four printings of *Mador of the Moor* appeared, two in Britain and two in the United States. In Britain, after the first edition published by Blackwood and Murray in 1816, the poem next appeared in Archibald Constable's four-volume edition of Hogg's *Poetical Works* (Edinburgh, 1822). Across the Atlantic, *Mador* was published first in Philadelphia by Moses Thomas in 1816, and then in New York in the 1825 two-volume *Poetical Works*. To the best of this editor's knowledge, neither manuscript nor proofs exist.

A collation of the four editions which were published during Hogg's lifetime reveals significant changes and revisions as well as the usual accidental (that is, non-verbal) changes. This edition's Note on the Text discusses the various changes and revisions to *Mador* in detail, and also sets out the reasons why it adopts the first edition (1816) as its copy-text. This choice of copy-text is important, for the poem as published by Blackie & Son in Glasgow in 1865 and as reprinted by AMS in 1973 reproduces a text based on the 1822 Edinburgh edition. The result is that Hogg's major themes and concerns are either short-circuited, thwarted, or truncated by printing changes. The most important omission is the lengthy 'Harper's Song' (containing 'The Song of the Fairies') which was excised from the 1822 Edinburgh edition and thus does not appear in the texts subsequently read and studied. Without these important passages the poem is not only modified, but seriously weakened.

During 1816 and 1817, reviews of *Mador of the Moor* appeared in at least ten publications, ranging from the *Scots Magazine* to the *Anti-Jacobin Review* and the *Eclectic Review*.[9] In format and content the reviews are typical of early nineteenth-century criticism, for they contain numerous lengthy quotations, long plot summaries, and generalisations about poetic strengths and weaknesses. For the most part this poem escapes the politically-charged reviewing which characterises so much of the early criticism of Romantic poets such as Coleridge, Byron, Shelley, and Keats.

Significantly, several of the reviewers recognize that Hogg's *Mador of the Moor* must be read against the background of Scott's *The Lady of the Lake* (1810). In one of the earliest reviews, the writer for the *Scots Magazine* says, 'There are pretty evident symptoms of its [the poem's] having been suggested, perhaps unconsciously, by Mr Scott's *Lady of the Lake*' (p. 449). And the *Critical Review* says that the 'new poem by Mr. Hogg, the Ettricke Shepherd, [...] is obviously an imitation of the style of Mr. Walter Scott, whose numerous and interesting productions have attracted so much notice, and upon which the critical powers of reviewers on both sides have been so often employed' (p. 131). But this reviewer does not find Scott a poet of the first rank, and Hogg, as his imitator, is not highly valued (p. 132). The *British Lady's Magazine* finds that *Mador of the Moor*, 'as a tale, cannot be prized for its originality; being a kind of second-hand "Lady of the Lake" in its construction' (p. 252). The writer for the *Literary Panorama* also thinks that the plot of the poem bears 'some resemblance to that adopted in the Lady of the Lake' (p. 740). Finally, the *Anti-Jacobin Review* notes that 'Mador of the Moor is written, if not in imitation, in the style and manner, of Mr. Walter Scott's poetical productions' (p. 328).

The five-canto structure of *Mador* produces some discussion as well. Several of the reviewers believe that Hogg ought to stick to the ballad and not attempt more sophisticated forms of poetry. The advice in the *Scots Magazine* is blunt:

> This attempt to produce a regular and classical poem—these fetters which the poet has imposed on himself, appear to us to divest his composition of much of its beauty.—He labours with difficulty, but in vain, to reach that equal and well-supported majesty which the subject and the rhythm demand; while these check him in those wild and airy flights, which form the great charm of his poetry. (p. 449)

The reviewer for the *Champion* also argues that Hogg should stay with the ballad style 'in which he greatly excels' and objects to Hogg's five-canto structure which leads to obscurity and mysteriousness (p. 182). However, the *Critical Review* writer finds Hogg's use of five cantos 'ingenious', for 'the reader is kept in interesting suspense as to the catastrophe' (pp. 134–35). These early reviewers recognized immediately that *Mador of the Moor* was a departure for Hogg and represented a new phase in his development. Moreover, although opinion is divided, the critics are aware that the five-canto structure is significant, but they do not explain why or how.

On the positive side, several reviewers recognise and appreciate Hogg's ability to write excellent descriptive nature poetry. Without much comment, the writer for the *Scots Magazine* quotes at length the introductory stanzas on the River Tay (pp. 449–50). The critic for the *Champion* also praises Hogg's nature descriptions, but notes that Hogg has the ability to 'rise higher than mere description, and natural imagery' (p. 182). In general, however, these reviewers provide little analysis of Hogg's language and his talent for evoking place. One of the most incisive comments appears in the *Champion*, which was edited by John Scott, who in 1821 died as a result of a duel which arose out of a dispute with Sir Walter Scott's son-in-law John Gibson Lockhart. In 1816 John Scott had tried to recruit Hogg as a contributor to the *Champion*: see Hogg's letter to John Scott of 28 February 1816. According to the *Champion*'s reviewer of *Mador*, Hogg 'must be a poet of considerable rank. He has much original genius' (p. 181). Praising Hogg's 'close-eyed observations of nature and his love of it' and comparing Hogg favourably with Wordsworth, Moore, Byron, and Coleridge, the *Champion* critic quotes at length and concludes, 'Mr. H. seems quite at home in the fields' (p. 182).

However, nearly all of the reviewers express significant reservations about *Mador of the Moor*. And even their praise contains damning insinuations. First, some critics find the supernatural elements in the poem a serious problem. The critic for the *British Lady's Magazine*, for example, complains, 'The waste of brilliant powers upon legendary fiction so exclusively, we consider a great evil, and begin to be heartily weary of the whole gothic mythology, and especially the half-told, half-hinted horrors of the hobgoblins of the middle ages' (p. 253). This writer does like the fairy song, but he objects that it is 'too long, and difficult to understand' (p. 254). The writer for the *Scots Magazine*, on the other hand, endorses 'the wild and sweet mythology' (p. 448), but this writer may not have read the poem carefully, for he asserts, 'It is a mere mortal story: all the principal agents are human; and there is scarcely even any supernatural machinery employed' (p. 449).

Secondly, several reviewers, either explicitly or implicitly, set firm limits on the poetic ambitions appropriate for a self-educated Scottish farm-worker. Although the reviewer for the *Scots Magazine* praises Hogg's 'expression of genuine Scottish feelings', even this critic believes Hogg is 'attempting a style which appears to him higher than that which he was wont to cultivate' and thus 'has missed the true sphere in which his excellence consists' (pp. 448–49). Even more condescending is the *Critical Review*, which asserts that Hogg 'as a native of Scotland, [is] probably not very well acquainted with our literature' and 'could not be supposed to possess that wide and perfect knowledge of the language which such a reduplication of sounds requires' (p. 143). More positive, but still condescending, is the commentator in the *British Lady's Magazine*, who observes that Hogg 'is another of the honourable instances furnished by Scotland of the noble fruits that may sometimes result from subordinate education' (p. 252). The *Anti-Jacobin Review* is more pointed: Hogg 'wants judgment, and, above all, he wants the knowledge of what is pleasing to an English ear, and gratifying to an English taste' (p. 329); this reviewer censures the 'uncouth jargon of the harpers' [*sic*] and fairies' songs' and urges, probably correctly, that a glossary of terms would help the readers unfamiliar with Scots (p. 330). And the *Critical Review* complains that the 'long harper's song [...] must be totally unintelligible to all who are not master of the rudest dialects of Scotland' (p. 136). Throughout these reviews runs an important thread: Hogg is Scottish and lower class; he has talent, but he is tainted by Northern qualities and will never find a secure place in the English literary tradition. The *Anti-Jacobin Review* provides this summation: 'His great error appears to be the substitution, in many places, of vulgar familiarity, for rustic simplicity; and the frequent use of terms unintelligible by all but Scotchmen' (p. 335).

The spectrum of contemporaneous critical opinion of *Mador of the Moor* can be illustrated by two critics, a writer for the *British Critic* in January 1817 and the critic for the *Eclectic Review* in February 1817. The first compares Hogg favourably with Burns in words which must have pleased Hogg: 'There is a native sweetness, a dignified simplicity in all the writings of Hogg, which Burns himself scarce attained' (p. 97). This critic concludes his article: 'If this poem be not read much and much admired, we shall think ill of the taste of the age' (p. 100). On the other hand, the *Eclectic Review* writer, while acknowledging that the critic and the public must always be ready to admit new forms of poetry, proclaims that 'as a whole, we think the poem is not good in any respect' (p. 175).

The Ettrick Shepherd and the Marginalised Poet

As some of the variants in the texts suggest and as the review of the critical reception of Hogg's *Mador* supports, Hogg was writing, as he well knew, from the point of view of the marginalised author. The text of the Edinburgh *Poetical Works* of 1822 'cleans up' the text of this self-educated and lower-class author, in part by removing the extremely important elements written in what Hogg called his 'ancient stile'.[10] In light of the reviews of the first edition, concern for commercial success probably dictated these decisions. However, a paradox exists, for Hogg and his publishers knew that one of the primary attractions of Hogg was his Ettrick Shepherd persona. Hogg realised and, indeed, cultivated his image as a direct spiritual descendent of Robert Burns, even coming to believe that he, like Burns, was born on 25 January, when in fact the parish register records his baptism as 9 December 1770. Hogg explains that upon hearing 'Tam o' Shanter' recited in 1797, his life was changed:

> This formed a new epoch of my life. Every day I pondered on the genius and fate of Burns. I wept, and always thought with myself—what is to hinder me from succeeding Burns? I too was born on the 25th of January, and I have much more time to read and compose than any ploughman could have, and can sing more old songs than ever ploughman could in the world. But then I wept again because I could not write. However, I resolved to be a poet, and to follow in the steps of Burns. ('Memoir', p. 18)

Whether Hogg is exaggerating or reconstructing is not at issue here, for even if he is fictionalising or refashioning the event, Hogg clearly sees himself as Burns's successor. Writing about his feelings fifteen years later, in 1812, Hogg remarks, 'I had an inward consciousness that I should yet live to be compared with Burns; and though I might never equal him in some things, I thought I might excel him in others' ('Memoir', p. 18). But if Hogg saw himself in that class of untutored native geniuses which included Burns, the Rev. Stephen Duck, and Ann Yearsley, the poetical washerwoman, he also knew that the price of admission to the literary elite—whether in Edinburgh or in London—would not be met by emphasising his rural or provincial heritage alone. Although in his 'Memoir' he does not complain of John Wilson's characterisations of him in the famous 'Noctes Ambrosianae', which appeared in *Blackwood's Edinburgh Magazine*, Hogg does complain about the *Noctes* in his letters,[11] and he must have been aware that he had helped create the situation in which he found himself. The very qualities of rural and untutored genius which made him popular and gave him fame were those which closed the door to the inner circle.

Contemporary accounts support this position. Bernard Barton, the Quaker Poet from Suffolk, praised Hogg in a poem which was used to preface the second edition of *The Queen's Wake*, but Barton himself remained on the literary periphery. Hogg's understanding of his position as viewed by Wordsworth is underscored in the Scot's account of an evening at Rydal Mount, Wordsworth's home. In addition to Wordsworth and Hogg, John Wilson ('Christopher North'), Charles Lloyd, and Thomas De Quincey were present. According to Hogg, 'there was a resplendent arch across the zenith, from the one horizon to the other, of something like the aurora borealis, but much brighter'. Dorothy Wordsworth, walking arm in arm with Hogg, expressed concern that the display 'might prove ominous'. Hogg responded, 'Hout, me'm! it is neither mair nor less than joost a treeumphal airch, raised in honour of the meeting of the poets' ('Memoir', p. 68).

Hogg goes on to assert that John Wilson thought this response good, but that Wordsworth objected to Hogg placing himself in the company of poets:

> Wordsworth, who had De Quincey's arm, gave a grunt, and turned on his heel, and leading the little opium-chewer aside, he addressed him in these disdainful and venomous words:— "Poets? Poets?—What does the fellow mean?—Where are they?" [...] The "*Where are they?*" was too bad! I have always some hopes that De Quincey was *leeing*, for I did not myself hear Wordsworth utter the words. ('Memoir', p. 68)

In this incident as well as in other contemporary reactions, Hogg was aware that being invited to the dinner table did not mean other diners thought he was more than a curiosity. True, John Gibson Lockhart defended Hogg in the *Quarterly Review* of 1831, insisting that Wilson's characterisation of Hogg as a 'boozing buffoon' was fallacious.[12] Nevertheless, Hogg's undeserved reputation as a drunken, uncouth, uncivilised primitive from north of the Border followed him, and in some ways he encouraged this reputation, for it gained him access to the periphery of some circles. On his visit to London, for example, 'he courted publicity by wearing a shepherd's plaid, and throughout his life he frequently referred to himself as "the Ettrick Shepherd" '.[13] Early in his 'Memoir' he says, 'I was a sort of natural songster, without another advantage on earth' (p. 24).

The theme of the marginalised poet appears in *Mador of the Moor*, but also in Hogg's earlier poems. For example, Hogg's obsession with the idea of the poet as outsider can be found in *The Queen's Wake* (1813), a poem in which his picture of a primitive shepherd-bard manages to tug on several cords to build sympathy for himself. While admitting the coarseness and unpolished character of the Tenth Bard,[14] Hogg also stresses an innate nobility which lifts the shepherd-poet above his station. Hogg's bard suffers, not from lack of talent, but lack of money. *Pilgrims of the Sun* (1815) provides additional insight into Hogg's mind and confirms that he was struggling with problems which were introduced first in *The Queen's Wake* (1813) and are explained more fully in *Mador of the Moor*. In the characterisation of a bard who 'keeps from the bustle of Border war',[15] rather devoting himself to his art and his vocation, singing and shepherding, Hogg explores another option: forsaking the powerful cultural elite for a romanticised life lived in rural society.

In *Mador of the Moor*, Hogg introduces again the poet on the fringe of society, but here the minstrel creates his own space, is master of his fate, and accepts full responsibility for his actions. The King, disguised as Mador the wandering minstrel, conflates two heroes from Scottish history: the fourteenth-century Robert II, the first Stuart king, and his sixteenth-century Stuart successor James V. In Canto I, Mador is called the 'Stuart' (I, l. 168),[16] an allusion to the account of Robert II in *The Scottish Chronicle*, a source frequently used by Hogg.[17] According to that account, before his marriage to the daughter of Hugh, Earl of Ross, Robert II had a mistress, Elizabeth Mure, who bore him two sons. Upon the death of his wife, he married this former mistress and legitimised their children, a decision paralleled in Hogg's poem. The other model for Mador's life and character, James V of Scotland, reputedly enjoyed disguising himself as a beggar and touring the countryside anonymously. Nineteenth-century Scots would have known legends of how James, eager to see that justice was administered and that the lower and oppressed classes were being looked after, frequently travelled incognito.[18] As Murray Pittock demonstrates in his edition of the Second Series of Hogg's *Jacobite Relics*, numerous ballads that predate *Mador of the Moor* allude to this tradition. Among Jacobite song groups, a 'Highland Laddie', who is sometimes James but more frequently Charles, appears as the patriotic spirit of the Highlander. In these lost-lover songs, a woman who represents Scotland leaves behind the corrupt 'pride of pelf' of Unionist Scotland for emotional and national liberty. According to Pittock, the songs appear to be related to the 'hidden prince' tradition found in several ballads that celebrate a gaberlunzie recognized by a woman (Scotland) who sees him for what he is, a merciful and quasi-divine member of a royal family. Pittock believes that these traditions, attached to James V, merged with the virile imagery of the Highland / gipsy abduction song to form a popular and powerful song-cycle with many variants. Their popularity extended to London where 'Gypsy-Laddie' songs were being sold by the early eighteenth century.[19]

Sir Walter Scott employs the figure of James V disguised as FitzJames in *The Lady of the Lake* (1810).[20] Hogg discusses this poem in no. 40 of his short-lived periodical *The Spy*, published on 1 June 1811. After opening the number with a quotation from the first canto of *The Lady of the Lake*,[21] Hogg writes a traveller's narrative in the voice of 'Malise', Roderick Dhu's henchman in Scott's poem. In this narrative, Hogg offers a critique of *The Lady of the Lake* which is significant for consideration of *Mador of the Moor*.

> I cannot help remarking here, Mr. Spy, that I think the greatest fault attached to the delightful poem of the *Lady of the Lake*, is, its containing no one fact, on which the mind of the enraptured peruser can rest as the basis of a principle so inherent in the human mind, as is the desire of affixing the stamp of reality on such incidents as interest us. The soul of man thirsts naturally and ardently for truth; and the author that ceases to deceive us with the appearance of it, ceases in a proportional degree to interest our feelings in behalf of the characters which he describes, or the fortunes of the individuals to which these characters are attached. [...] In this poem he never once leaves the inchanting field of probability, yet the mind is forced reluctantly to acknowledge, that it has been pursuing an illusion, and interesting itself in a professed fiction. The *possibility*, is not even left of attaching the idea of truth to one event, which might have served as a pivot on which the rest would have turned; with which we would gladly have associated every other circumstance, and acquiesced with delight in the delicious deception. I admire the easy and simple majesty of that sweet tale as much as any person can possibly do; but I have never read it without regretting, that it had not been founded on a fact, though ever so trivial; and though my taste may be particular in this matter, I felt the effect rather distressing to reflection on viewing every scene of action referred to in the poem, which causes me to mention it in this place.
> (*The Spy*, p. 398)

The Lady of the Lake is a metrical romance, and in this passage Hogg suggests that Scott has not done enough to anchor his poem in reality. This assertion provides a context for the final stanza of the Introduction of *Mador of the Moor*, in which Hogg writes that, as 'Nature's simple Bard', he will not write of 'men all pure, and maidens all divine', but his concern (more realistically) will be with 'those whose virtues and defects combine, | Such as in erring man we daily see– | The child of failings born, and scathed humanity'.

Scott and Hogg were great friends, and Hogg often visited and talked with Scott about works in progress. In several ways, Hogg's *Mador of the Moor* seems to be in dialogue with his friend's longer and more famous poem, but the dialogue is extremely subtle and canny. Like *Mador*, *The Lady of the Lake* begins with a hunt. In both poems, deer run, dogs give chase, and noble hunters in disguise become guests. In Scott's poem, FitzJames visits the Lady of the Lake; in Hogg's poem, Mador spends several days and nights with Kincraigy and his family. Beyond these obvious parallels, in some significant respects Hogg is deliberately responding to and calling into question Scott's characterisation of James V. In Scott's poem, the king returns to Stirling Castle, takes up residence, and accepts the homage of his courtiers and his countrymen. Even though at one point King James wonders why anyone would want to attempt to rule such an unruly lot, he eventually accepts his obligation and the privileged position of king. This ending corroborates Hogg's opinion that Scott was too committed to rank and station. Near the beginning of his *Familiar Anecdotes of Sir Walter Scott*, Hogg says,

> The only foible I ever could discover in the character of Sir Walter was a too strong leaning to the old aristocracy of the country. His devotion for titled rank was prodigious and in such an illustrious character altogether out of place.[22]

And Hogg, near the closing of his *Familiar Anecdotes*, reports in the same vein:

> The Whig ascendency in the British cabinet killed Sir Walter. Yes I say and aver it was that which broke his heart deranged his whole constitution and murdered him. [...] From the moment he percieved the veto of a democracy prevailing he lost all hope of the prosperity and ascendancy of the British empire. (*Anecdotes*, p. 73)

Certainly, the narrative and conclusion to *The Lady of the Lake* provides an idealised vision of nobility inherent in a man of title. FitzJames commits no immoral acts; he fights honourably in hand-to-hand combat—and wins. He endures hardships, loneliness, and rejection with equanimity. And he accepts, without question, a position which is his by heredity and birth.

In contrast, Hogg's king-disguised-as-minstrel, while hardy and resolute, exhibits human failings and foibles. He succumbs to the beauty of a country girl and the wiles of her mother; he suffers ignominious treatment by the girl's father; he is nearly killed in a brawl with the girl's other suitor (and is rescued by the girl herself); and he comes to see his duty only when called to account by the Abbot of Dunfermline, in a scene which recalls the visit of the prophet Samuel to King David in II Samuel 12. Hogg's situation as marginalised observer and poet allows him to enter into dialogue with Scott, but it also enables him to criticise his friend's positions. While Scott calls for both recognition and restoration of the aristocratic order, Hogg questions whether a staying action is feasible and desirable. Instead, Hogg suggests a reconstruction of society in which titled monarch-cum-bard, recognising his duties and obligations, refuses to create an artificial niche at court for the wronged heroine Ila Moore, but instead forges a new life for her and himself outside the court where Ila's natural, innate, and inherent nobility and goodness will not be called into question by the artificial standards of court life.

In addition to the narrative intertextuality of the two poems, verbal parallels in the texts occur frequently. For example, both poems are set in Perthshire. Describing the hunter's horse, Scott says, 'But lightly Bayard clears the lea' (V, stanza xvii, l. 32), which Hogg turns to 'Bayard and blood-hound now thy hope must be' (I, l. 80). And Scott's description of the hunted deer as 'antler'd monarch of the waste' (I, stanza ii, l. 3) may be echoed in Hogg's 'The antler'd rover sought his widow'd den' (I, l. 13). And both poems include in the first canto a ballad which illuminates the meaning and gives shape to the entire poem.

However, noting possible verbal parallels conceals rather than reveals the significance of the literary relationship between Hogg and Scott. As current criticism has acknowledged, Hogg was far from being a weak and inept imitator of Scott and other literary figures, and attentive reading of Hogg's texts against other texts opens up radically new understandings of both Hogg and those he was supposedly imitating. Careful reading of *Mador of the Moor* and *The Lady of the Lake* reveals that rather than imitating Scott, Hogg sought to question and revise the value system Scott espoused. In fact, Hogg appears to be suggesting a complete revision of the social order and

the principles which undergirded his society. Rather than support-
ing Scott's faith in the *noblesse oblige* tradition fostered and practised
by James V in *The Lady of the Lake*, Hogg insists that the natural
dignity and nobility of a peasant girl ought to be recognised by any
nobleman who faces honestly his own humanity and human nature
in general. Though Ila Moore bears a child out of wedlock, she
should be accorded a place of her own equal to that of the man who
fathered her son.

On another level, Hogg's poetic performance in *Mador* imagina-
tively challenges Scott's more famous *The Lady of the Lake*. Both po-
ems open with accounts of royal hunts. Dogs, deer, retainers, knights,
and monarchs appear and reappear as men strive to exhibit valour,
prowess, and skill. However, Scott's depiction of the hunt presents
a quasi-heraldic stylisation of the action, like a hunting scene woven
into a tapestry, which creates a distancing effect. Both in general and
in particular, Hogg's account of the hunt is more realistic and imme-
diately compelling; it is virile, frenzied, even bloody, and certainly
exhausting to read. The narrator creates the sounds, the feelings,
the hopes, and the disappointments of the hunt. Scott says, 'The
deep-mouthed blood-hound's heavy bay | Resounded up the rocky
way' (*Lady*, I, stanza i, ll. 7–8). In Hogg's hands, the baying of the
hound dominates the scene:

> Louder and fiercer, Jowler, unappall'd,
> Across the glen, along the mountain brawl'd,
> Unpractised he to part till blood was seen–
> Though sore by precipice and darkness gall'd,
> He turn'd his dewlap to the starry sheen,
> And howl'd in furious tone, with yelp and bay between.
> (I, ll. 157–62)

Another example underscores the differences between Scott's
technique, which is to talk about the event, and Hogg's approach,
which is to create the event so that the reader participates in the
action. Scott talks about the dogs, noise and excitement:

> An hundred dogs bayed deep and strong,
> Clattered an hundred steeds along,
> Their peal the merry horns rung out,
> An hundred voices joined the shout;
> With hark and whoop and wild halloo.
> (*Lady*, I, stanza iii, ll. 5–9)

In Hogg's poem the suspense grows, the circle of the hunt contracts, and the hunters break into cheers:

> The driver circle narrow'd on the heath,
>   Close, and more close, the deer were bounding bye;
> Upon the bow-string lies the shaft of death!
>   Breathless impatience burns in every eye!
>   At once a thousand winged arrows fly;
> The grayhound up the glen outstrips the wind;
>   At once the slow-hounds' music rends the sky,
> The hunter's whoop and hallo cheers behind!
> Haloo! away they speed! swift as the course of mind!
>   (I, ll. 64–72)

Besides offering an alternative poetic performance of the hunt, these passages also suggest that Hogg is jousting with Scott's reputation as the pre-eminent reporter of Border and Highland life. Scott's narrator observes; Hogg's narrator participates, emerging sweaty, thirsty, even blood-speckled.

Hogg's undeserved reputation as a weak and inept imitator of his literary betters can also be illustrated by comparing a passage from *Mador* about the hunting hound Jowler with Alexander Pope's account of Belinda's lapdog Shock from *The Rape of the Lock*. In Hogg's scene, the King of Scots has fallen asleep, but his sleep is disturbed by the vision of a beautiful woman:

> The heavenly guardian of the royal head,
>   That rules events and elements at will,
> Unused in wilderness to watch his bed,
>   Or spread his shelt'ring pinion on the hill,
>   Unrife in circumstance forboding ill,
> Yet trembled for some danger lingering near.
>   What gath'ring sound comes nigher, nigher still?
> Why does the wakening hound turn up his ear,
> Then start with shorten'd bark, and bristle all with fear?
>   (I, ll. 190–98)

In this passage, the royal head is disturbed by a vision of loveliness and the heavenly spirits which guard the monarch are distressed by the wilderness environment. They tremble out of anticipated danger, and the monarch's dog exhibits distress signs.

In Pope's famous opening canto of *The Rape of the Lock*, Belinda's guardian sylph Ariel is troubled by impending doom and tries to warn the coquette in her dreams, but the heavenly spirit is frustrated in this attempt by Belinda's vision of her lover. Ariel's long speech is interrupted when Belinda's lapdog Shock, 'who thought she slept too long, | Leaped up, and waked his mistress with his tongue' (I, ll. 115–16).[23]

That Hogg is drawing on Pope's poem seems beyond dispute.[24] But is he merely borrowing naively and inexpertly? In fact, Hogg has performed a difficult feat. He recalls a magnificent comic scene with which nearly all of his readers would have been familiar, and by recasting it in serious terms, he has turned a sequence which undercuts a set of values into a new narrative which affirms a set of values not unlike those which Pope questions.

Pope's poem, drawing on the epic tradition, plays the Enlightenment tune precisely. Belief in supernatural forces is archaic; reason ought to govern human behaviour; women at their worst are deluded by society's standards and thus easily betrayed. Hogg's dialogue with Pope cuts aslant. Although he does not confront Pope's value system directly (Hogg would not expect that much would be gained that way), he does suggest that while the supernatural may seem redundant as conceived in elite and learned society, those conceptions of the supernatural take on another character when uprooted and reassigned to guard the monarch in his wilderness bed. The flitting, visionary phantoms which disturb the sleep of people who live in the city have little in common with the real and tangible night sounds of the country. Belinda's docile, irreverent lapdog which ignores the supernatural and interrupts well-intended warnings is traded for the not-easily-troubled Jowler, a brave hound who exhibits great courage and fortitude, but who also respects the unnamed natural forces. Rather than borrowing indiscriminately, Hogg alludes deliberately and consciously to a well-known text in order to question the unspoken assumptions of the culture and to propose alternative structures for a post-Enlightenment existence.

As we have seen in the opening canto, Hogg implicitly questions Scott's elitist agenda for the future and criticises Pope's vision too. Another figure, John Milton, has a reflected voice in this conversation as well. In Canto One, the narrator describes the twilight landscape of the Grampian Mountains in conflicting terms:

> But O what bard could sing the onward sight!
>   The piles that frown'd, the gulfs that yawn'd beneath!
> Downward a thousand fathoms from the height,
>   Grim as the caverns in the land of death!
>   Like mountains shatter'd in th' Eternal's wrath,
> When fiends their banners 'gainst his reign unfurl'd—

A grisly wilderness! a land of scathe!
Rocks upon rocks in dire confusion hurl'd!
A rent and formless mass, the rubbish of a world.

As if by lost pre-eminence abashed,
    Hill behind hill erected locks of gray,
And every misty morion was upraised,
    To speak their farewell to the God of Day:
    When tempests rave along their polar way,
Not closer rear the billows of the deep,
    Shining with silver foam, and maned with spray,
As up the mid-way heaven they war and sweep,
Then, foil'd and chafed to rage, roll down the broken steep.
                                        (I, ll. 118–35)

In these stanzas, Milton's influence appears in both verbal over-
tones and specific references, such as 'When fiends their banners
'gainst his reign unfurl'd–' (I, l. 123), which is a clear allusion to the
rebellion of Satan and his angelic followers in *Paradise Lost*. Less
explicit verbal efforts also recall Milton's epic: 'gulfs that yawn'd',
'Downward a thousand fathoms from the height', 'Like mountains
shatter'd in th' Eternal's wrath', and 'As if by lost pre-eminence
abashed'. Hogg's purposes in this passage are complex and thought-
provoking. By invoking the greatest epic in the English language,
Hogg tells the reader that this is no trivial tale. He begins the de-
scription of the coming of night by asking what bard is capable of
capturing the conflict of day and night. In short, he appears to be
arguing that even Milton, who captured the conflict between good
and evil, could not accomplish this task, and indeed Hogg may even
be questioning his own skill. However, by elevating this immediate
task above the portrayal of the cosmic forces at work in *Paradise Lost*,
Hogg makes a significant point. The poetic challenge today is not to
'justify the ways of God to man', but to heighten the human percep-
tion of natural forces in conflict. While not wishing to diminish
Milton's achievement nor the significance of Milton's theme, Hogg
finds that the poetic task, which in his mind is of heroic proportions,
is to illuminate the clash of natural forces in the everyday world.

Hogg reconciles these disparate forces in the powerful imagina-
tive vision closing Stanza 16. Although light has been chased away
('No star along the firmament was seen'), chaos does not reign. In-
stead, 'solemn majesty' prevails. And evening, abbreviated and
anthropomorphised as Eve, referring perhaps to innocence both lost

and regained in the Edenic story, reigns in splendour on the mountains of Grampian (I, ll. 142–45).

In these reflected conversations with Scott, Pope, and Milton, Hogg's poem demonstrates an intellectual acumen which has not been adequately recognised. Unfortunately for his reputation, the persona which he cultivated as rustic poet of the Scottish Margins gained him admission to literary circles, but militated against his being taken seriously as a poet with a keen mind and talent. While enjoying the friendship of Scott, he demonstrates fundamental differences with his confidant and calls for a reordering of priorities and values. Although he respects the genius of Alexander Pope, Hogg emphasises that the intellectual frame of mind which dominates Pope's poetry is not appropriate for the challenges of the nineteenth century. And while Hogg knows that he cannot escape the influence of Milton, he reformulates the battle lines for the nineteenth-century mind. Early readers of Hogg, introduced to him through the eyes of the Edinburgh elite, tended to see only an impulse to imitate. Readers of today, conditioned by anxieties of influence, find not an imitator but one who by slaying his father prepares a new agenda.

The Literary Context

Hogg's poem has its inception in the descriptive and topographical poetic tradition, in which Scottish writers such as James Beattie and James Thomson excelled. His decision to use the Spenserian stanza not only refers back to the author of *The Shepheardes Calender* and *The Faerie Queene*, but also involves the eighteenth-century revival of this form in such influential Scottish poems as Thomson's *The Castle of Indolence* (1748), Beattie's *The Minstrel* (1771), and Burns's 'The Cotter's Saturday Night' (1786). Furthermore, Hogg would certainly be well aware of the powerful example provided by a very recent poem: Byron's *Childe Harold's Pilgrimage*, written in Spenserian stanzas, had been published in 1812 to general acclaim; and in his dedication to *The Corsair* (1814) Byron writes of the Spenserian stanza, 'I confess, it is the measure most after my own heart'.[25]

In Scottish literature, there is a 'Spenserian' tradition, which probably parallels the development of the Spenserian forms in English literature, but developed independently. For example, according to Kurt Wittig in *The Scottish Tradition in Literature*, many of the several hundred Scottish sonnets from the court of James VI are written 'in the "Spenserian" form—which Scottish poets used years before

Spenser'.[26] In addition, James Craigie, in *The Poems of James VI of Scotland*, argues that although Spenser may have seen a copy of James's *Essayes of a Prentise*, which contains sixteen sonnets employing the *abab bcbc cdcd ee* rhyme scheme now associated with Spenser, James's sonnets ante-dated Spenser by several years and their existence suggests a Spenserian tradition which evolved independently in Scotland.[27]

Students of prosody have often noted that the Spenserian stanza is the first eight lines of the Spenserian sonnet plus an additional hexameter. However, whether the sonnet or the stanza developed first has not been determined. James Craigie argues that Scottish poets were familiar with two examples of a stanza form which might be regarded as two decasyllabic quatrains bound together by an interlocking rhyme scheme. The first was the French *huictain* which Clement Marot favoured and which Montgomerie borrowed from Marot. The other was the stanza King James used in the eighth chapter of his *Reulis and Cautelis* and designated as 'Ballet Royal'. This form survived in Scotland in Middle Scots poems and enjoyed some popularity into the sixteenth century.[28]

This parallel 'Spenserian' tradition also emerges in the work of James Thomson, the most famous of the many Anglo-Scottish poets of the eighteenth century. Perhaps unfairly marginalised because they are at once too English and not sufficiently Scottish, according to Mary Jane Scott, they deserve closer reading, for like Hogg, they cannot escape being Scottish. As Mary Jane Scott says, 'Scottishness is a stubborn thing [...]. It is all those intangible influences—religious, historical, educational, aesthetic, geographical, linguistic, literary, and broadly cultural—which work together to determine national and individual character'.[29] Thomson, although frequently anthologised as a member of the English canon, exhibits qualities of the Scottish tradition, especially in his Spenserian efforts, which point towards Hogg and provide a foundation for *Mador of the Moor*.

Two of the qualities most admired in Thomson, atmosphere-painting and vivid impressions, are common in Scots poetry in general and in Hogg in particular. Also, the predilection for formal intricacy which finds expression in the Spenserian stanzas of both Thomson and Hogg is a feature of Scots poetry from Dunbar onwards.[30] Thomson expressed a love for wild nature, a familiarity with Scottish themes and traditions, and a fascination with elements of the supernatural, folk-life, and folklore. And he integrated these particulars into the intricate and formal Spenserian stanza. Hogg may have learned his craft from Thomson, for *The Castle of Indolence* contains a significant supernatural element and exaggerated diction, employing archaic language closely akin to Middle Scots.[31] In the earliest printing, as will be shown later in this introduction, Hogg's *Mador of the Moor* follows this Thomson model.

But Thomson was not the only Spenserian who flourished among eighteenth-century Scottish poets. As David Hill Radcliffe shows in his essay 'Crossing Borders: The Untutored Genius as Spenserian Poet', another landmark is provided by James Beattie's *The Minstrel*. According to Radcliffe, when 'the Spenserian stanza came into general usage between 1770 and 1830', several recognisable sequences of Spenserian poems emerged, 'including one concerned with self-taught writers'. Radcliffe continues:

> This topic was started by Thomas Gray's account of a 'mute inglorious Milton', a village poet condemned to silence for lack of education in the classics. In *The Minstrel, or The Progress of Genius*, James Beattie responded to Gray by describing the education of a village poet whose natural faculties develop through extra-curricular encounters with nature, folklore, and visionary experiences. [...] In the half-century following the publication of Beattie's *Minstrel* in 1771 provincial writers, and in particular unlettered poets, produced a large body of literary poetry based not on classical sources but on canonical English models—sometimes Spenser and Milton, but more often eighteenth-century poets, Goldsmith and Beattie perhaps chief among them. Beattie rather than Spenser was the point of departure for most of the writers I will discuss; *The Minstrel* disseminated ideals of poetic genius, descriptive vividness, and simplicity of tone to many writers unfamiliar with Spenser.[32]

Clearly, when *Mador of the Moor* follows Beattie in adopting the Spenserian stanza, Hogg's decision connects with his desire (as a self-taught poet) to assert the potential worth of a poetry based on 'encounters with nature, folklore, and visionary experiences' rather than classical learning. In a well-known passage in his *Familiar Anecdotes of Sir Walter Scott*, Hogg records a conversation with Scott in which he refused to accept Scott's assertion that they were both of the same school as poets:

> "Dear Sir Walter ye can never suppose that I belang to your school o' chivalry? Ye are the king o' that school but I'm the king o' the mountain an' fairy school which is a far higher ane nor yours." (*Anecdotes*, p. 61)

Hogg's concept of 'the mountain an' fairy school' was manifestly based on a desire to draw on and articulate the values and traditions of his native Ettrick community, but it also connects with the widespread tradition of poems influenced by *The Minstrel*, a tradition whose features (according to Radcliffe) include 'Spenserian stanzas, descriptions of nature or domestic life, reiteration of ballads, fairy poetry, archaisms and the like'.[33]

A related desire to assert the worth of the rural poor emerges in another famous Scottish poem of the late eighteenth century written in Spenserian stanzas, Burns's 'The Cotter's Saturday Night'. Like the cotter's family, Hogg's Ila Moore exhibits genuine worth, intelligence, and nobility in her poverty, and *Mador of the Moor* connects with reading patterns and a Scottish Spenserian tradition into which Hogg deliberately sought to tap. As Jonathan Rose has shown in his *The Intellectual Life of the British Working Classes*, the lower classes throughout the eighteenth and nineteenth centuries incorporated the most elite and difficult works of the Western tradition into their daily lives. Weavers, fisherman, and miners read and studied the tradition from Shakespeare to Carlyle.[34] The contemporary critical fear that 'high culture' is anti-democratic and preserves ideological power relationships, thus undermining egalitarian impulses, may be misplaced and exaggerated, according to Rose. Seen in this context, Hogg's employment of the Spenserian stanza and the minstrel tradition in *Mador of the Moor* may indicate more than simple imitation of an intricate rhyme scheme or even a decision to join an already long Scottish tradition of Spenserian writing. As this introduction shows later, Hogg probably realised that his stanzaic pattern would provide him with a golden opportunity to raise the profile of folk culture, and to assert the potential worth of self-educated writers.

In writing *Mador*, Hogg clearly believed that the new age called for a new kind of poem. Evidence of this exists in his recording of Eliza Izett's challenge to him to write. A suspicious reader might caution that Hogg is deliberately referring to William Cowper's taking up the gauntlet laid down by Lady Austen, which culminated in *The Task*, a long, recursive and descriptive poem; yet Hogg argues both in his 'Memoir' and in *Mador* for new artistic strategies. Hogg's account of the origin of *Mador of the Moor* ('Memoir', pp. 34–35) makes clear that he was reluctant merely to write a long, descriptive poem. Even so, in the 1810s the genre of the descriptive poem was still alive and well. In fact, Hogg would have to have been acutely aware of the topographical / descriptive poem from Pope's *Windsor Forest* (1713) through James Thomson's *The Seasons* (published and

enlarged over sixteen years from 1726 to 1742) to Cowper's *The
Task* (1785). Between 1730 and 1800 Thomson's immensely popu-
lar poem was printed fifty times, greatly influencing the Romantics.
Hogg may even have been familiar with Wordsworth's first excur-
sions into descriptive nature poetry, 'An Evening Walk' and 'De-
scriptive Sketches'. Choosing the Spenserian stanza, which he de-
scribes as 'the finest verse in the world' because 'it rolls off with
such majesty and grandeur' was important to his strategy: 'What an
effect it will have in the description of mountains, cataracts, and
storms!' ('Memoir', p. 35). Hogg concludes his account of the ori-
gins of *Mador of the Moor* as follows:

> I was fond of the Spenserian measure; but there was some-
> thing in the best models that always offended my ear. It was
> owing to this. I thought it so formed, that every verse ought to
> be a structure of itself, resembling an arch, of which the two
> meeting rhymes in the middle should represent the key-stone,
> and on these all the strength and flow of the verse should rest.
> On beginning this poem, therefore, I had the vanity to believe
> that I was going to give the world a new specimen of this
> stanza in its proper harmony. It was under these feelings that
> my poem "Mador of the Moor" was begun, and in a very
> short time completed: but I left out to the extent of one whole
> book of the descriptive part. There is no doubt whatever that
> my highest and most fortunate efforts in rhyme are contained
> in some of the descriptions of nature in that poem, and in the
> "Ode to Superstition" in the same measure. ('Memoir', p. 35)

Thomson is a key figure in eighteenth-century Scottish and Brit-
ish poetry, and for *Mador of the Moor*. He is recognised, appropri-
ately, for his ability to teach the reader to see and to feel, taking as
his subject 'the general effects of light and cloud and foliage or the
particular image of a leaf tossed in the gale or the slender feet of a
robin on the delicate film of ice at the edge of a brook'.[35] Thomson
generalizes and particularizes, while Hogg also localizes the particu-
lars, describing nature and landscapes in specific detail. Whether he
is concerned with a place such as a house or a mountain or an ani-
mal, Hogg's tendency is to observe at the level of the particular, an
approach owing more to the first canto of Scott's *The Lay of the Last
Minstrel* (1805) than to Thomson. In *Mador*, Hogg's sense of place is
finely attuned, geographical references are precise. He is not so much
concerned with 'the general effects of light and cloud and foliage' as
in the effects of light and cloud and foliage in the particular land-

scape of Perthshire. The generic robin or daffodil does not interest him so much as the particularised dew-bell or ptarmigan, species native to the landscape of this poem. In the following passage, he resembles Thomson:

> O'er reddening moors, and wilds of soften'd gray,
> The youthful swain, unfashion'd, unendow'd,
> The brocket and the lamb may round thee play:
> These thy first guest alone, thou fair, majestic Tay!
> (Introduction, ll. 33–36)

At other times and in other situations, especially when he writes about particular places, he expresses his individual vision more successfully: 'From cairn of Bruar to the dark Glen-More, | The forest's in a howl, and all is wild uproar!' (I, ll. 8–9). An even better example of his skill, especially for readers familiar with the region, is stanza 11 in Canto I:

> The Tilt is vanish'd on the upland gray,
> The Tarf is dwindled to a foaming rill;
> But many a hound lay gasping by the way,
> Bathed in the stream, or stretch'd upon the hill;
> The cooling brook with burning jaws they swill,
> Nor once will deign to scent the tainted ground:
> The herd has cross'd Breriach's gulfing gill,
> The Athol forest's formidable bound,
> And in the Garcharye a last retreat have found.
> (I, ll. 91–99)

Hogg does more than mention exact names of rivers in the Perthshire region such as the Tilt and the Tarf. He also gives descriptions accurate to the minute detail. He knows where the rivers have their origins. He is familiar with the size of 'Breriach's gulfing gill', the intimidating qualities of the Atholl forest, and the safe refuges to be found in Garcharye. Hogg does not use rivers as set pieces; he conjures up the concrete and specific Tilt and Tarf.

Hogg's sense of place includes the actual sites of Kinnaird House and Kincraigy. Kinnaird House has been enlarged and remodelled several times in the century and a half since Hogg reportedly began *Mador* there, but as in Hogg's day the nearby Kincraigy still sits high above the River Tay, facing not the valley, but the hills and glens. The poem's initial description of Ila Moore's home is firmly rooted in the real landscape Hogg encountered in his visits to the Izetts: 'Far mountains mixing with aërial gray, | Low golden-vested vallies stretch'd between, | And far below the eye, broad flood and islet green' (II, ll. 68–72).

The modern Kincraigy is a modest farmhouse, surrounded by several cottages which are now holiday rentals. In the nineteenth century it would have been a substantial if not a sumptuous house. As the narrator in Hogg's poem makes clear, Ila Moore's father, also known as 'Kincraigy' in accordance with traditional Scottish usage, was a prosperous farmer with aspirations to ascend the social ladder by marrying his daughter to the land-owning Albert of the Glen. Describing Kincraigy, the narrator comments, 'He was not man of rank, nor mean degree' (II, l. 5); and later the reader is told that 'Her sire was liegeman bound, and held of him his all' (II, l. 36). The house of Kincraigy as it now stands still can be imagined as reflecting those ambitions, for it clearly dominates the surrounding cottages. The back of the house, which faces the Tay Valley, is severe, but protects the inhabitants from the frigid northeasterly winds. Between the house and the distant Tay are long stretches of descending fields and valleys. The front door, which faces west and looks up to the near hills, provides a sheltered entrance and a lovely prospect. In producing his own sharply particularised version of this setting, Hogg differs from his predecessors like Thomson and even some of his contemporaries whose nature descriptions, in keeping with eighteenth-century privileging of the universal over the particular, are devoid of precise detail and evoke feelings based on generalisations.

Themes and Structure

Readers of Hogg's *Mador of the Moor* should not be faulted for seldom recognizing the complexity and subtlety of the poem. Hampered by reprintings of a corrupt text which eliminated important passages in the first canto and prejudiced by assumptions that Hogg merely imitated his betters, readers and scholars have relegated Hogg's poem to a minor place in the history of letters. However, reading the restored text with close attention to the five-canto structure of the poem reveals a work of surprising depth and nuances.

First, Hogg's permutations on the five-canto structure are unusual, perhaps unique. Unlike Pope's *The Rape of the Lock*, *Mador of the Moor* does not maintain a single focus and a linear movement. Pope's narrator takes a panoramic perspective. The action, although it parodies epic characteristics, moves essentially from one event to the next in strict chronological order. Hogg's artistic strategy is different. He provides an overview of the entire story in Canto I, but the cantos are strictly organised to emphasize the major themes of the poem.

Canto I, entitled 'The Hunting', consists of forty-two stanzas plus the lengthy 'Harper's Song', and is written from the point of view of the omniscient, objective narrator. It focuses on the activities of the court and the monarch. The royal hunt is foregrounded, but the Harper's mysterious lay which celebrates local customs and super-stition as well as the promise of a new way of relating to the world is the focal point of the canto. Unfortunately, this minstrel's song has often been omitted in reprintings of the poem, and as a result the poem has sometimes been misunderstood. In Canto I, Hogg em-ploys the widest-possible lens. He passes over some narrative ele-ments such as Mador's visit to Kincraigy and provides the broadest possible sweep, whetting the reader's appetite for the full story while focusing on the events as seen from the perspective of the King's retainers, followers, and companions.

Canto II, called 'The Minstrel' and consisting of fifty-six stanzas, retains the same narrative voice as Canto I, but fills in some of the missing narrative elements from Canto I. However, the action is viewed from the perspective of the inhabitants of the hamlet of Kincraigy as well as the man Kincraigy and his family. The lens angle is more focused, the action restricted to the environs of Kincraigy and the River Tay. Emphasising the character of Kincraigy, his wife, and his daughter, Hogg also stresses the travelling minstrel's behaviour, talents, and visits. The events are described as the people of the Kincraigy hamlet would have seen them.

In Canto III, which is titled 'The Cottage', the focus becomes even more concentrated and restricted. The point of view is intimate and narrow. Containing only twenty-eight stanzas, this short canto, while revealing more about the characters of Kincraigy, his wife, and his daughter, resembles a nativity scene. It is as though Mary and the Christ Child, abandoned by Joseph, have sought refuge with Mary's parents.

Canto IV, consisting of thirty-nine stanzas, is named appropri-ately 'The Palmer', for it recounts Ila Moore's pilgrimage to 'Strevline' (Stirling) in her search for the child's father and the ac-tions of the Palmer who supports, encourages, and protects the pil-grim pair. The movement and action of this canto provide a counter-point to the stability and stasis of Canto III, but it is even more restricted in focus, for the Palmer, Ila Moore, and the child are the centre of attention.

Canto V contains thirty-five stanzas. Titled 'The Christening', this canto does not in fact focus on the child, but on Ila Moore. Although the Abbot of Dunfermline plays a significant role and Kincraigy is reunited with daughter and grandson, Ila Moore is the centre of attention. She is viewed from several perspectives—the penitent, the seeker, and eventually the redeemed one. Elevated to her well-deserved status as partner to the monarch, she sits in regal splendour, rewarded for her honesty, integrity, sincerity, and inherent goodness. Ila Moore is the dominant figure in Canto V, and the camera has only her in focus.

Hogg's narrative talents have seldom been clearer. He provides a plot outline in the first canto while retaining the reader's interest by omitting relevant details and stressing strong narrative action in the royal hunt. In succeeding cantos, he provides missing details, reveals complexities in the main characters, resolves the plot, and gradually limits the focus from canto to canto until finally Ila Moore is pre-eminent—and even Mador is in the background. As a result, Hogg clarifies his major themes of a new social order in which forgiveness is practised and innate goodness and nobility are recognized. In addition, making Ila Moore the centre of the action and focusing on her, especially in Cantos III through V, underscores Hogg's reconstruction of society's values and order. As a result, Hogg redefines the role of women in society, for Ila Moore not only experiences grace and forgiveness, but takes a prominent place, not as an appendage to a royal husband but as a partner with her husband in a new environment outside the confines and hierarchy of the court.

Unfortunately, Hogg's theme of grace and forgiveness has been obscured by textual corruption. Beginning with the 1822 Edinburgh edition and in the most used reprints or reissues of the poem, 'The Harper's Song', a crucial segment from Canto I, has been omitted, perhaps because the language is difficult for English readers, probably in an effort to downplay the rustic and vulgar characteristics of *Mador of the Moor*: this topic is explored in greater detail in the present edition's Appendix I, on 'The Harper's Song'. At all events, 'The Harper's Song' employs numerous obscure words and obsolete phrases, and non-Scottish readers may be tempted to overlook the song's significance or even to think it an interlude and, therefore, irrelevant to the narrative. However, 'The Harper's Song' announces and describes a central focus of the poem: the ancient rites and superstitions arising out of prehistory are replaced by the experience of grace and salvation celebrated by the new Christian faith. 'The

Harper's Song' sketches this development, which is then writ large in the action of the full poem. In the song, the narrator first introduces a weathered old man (an allegorical representation of 'Superstition') who has confronted daily the vicissitudes of human experience. However, the narrator insists that the old man no longer walks the hills and valleys alone, for he is now accompanied by a meek and beautiful child who is an allegorical representation of heavenly Grace (I, ll. 292–93). In addition to having a beautiful countenance which radiates peace, the child wears a stunning rainbow-coloured snood or headband and a cloak as white as new snow. Her beauty inspires the fairies to sing a new song which reorients the natural world (I, ll. 312–19). The eight-stanza 'Song of the Fairies' celebrates the child and her effects on nature, humans, and society. The fairies praise the infant's ability to disperse dark spirits and to drive water sprites into hiding. As in 'Kilmeny' in *The Queen's Wake*, the result is a new creation, a kind of new order, a land where the faerie springtime is ever new. The child's impact is not merely beneficent or beneficial. Rather, all that she influences experience a kind of new creation. They no longer experience darkness, disorder, and decay. They no longer are subject to fear, confusion, and death. Arguably, the final canto of Hogg's poem ('The Christening') shows similarly redemptive consequences flowing from the conduct of Ila Moore, the unmarried mother as heroine.

In the conclusion to 'The Harper's Song', after the fairies have flown off to a land of bliss and holy silence (I, ll. 407–08), the old man kneels and names the child 'Grace' as the light of God strikes his face (I, ll. 421–44). In this significant passage, Hogg drives home a major tenet: when Grace enters human experience, nature, society, and human beings are transformed. Nature is made over into a new creation which is peopled by new creatures who live in a different kind of society.

Within this poem, Hogg acknowledges the pervasive power of the ancient beliefs and refuses to dismiss their influence or to denigrate the power of supernatural belief. In both the Introduction and Conclusion, which serve as bookends supporting the five cantos of *Mador*, the poet affirms the existence of familiar practices and tenacious beliefs. If the Introduction expresses nostalgia and longing for the 'sacred fount' and 'haunted tree' which inspire even as they represent a dying belief system, the Conclusion combines an acknowledgment of the existence of fairy superstition with a longing for the poet's native Ettrick and Yarrow in the Borders and a place for eventual recognition as an authentic poetic voice:

RETURN, my Harp, unto the Border dale,
   Thy native green hill, and thy fairy ring;
No more thy murmurs on the Grampian gale
   May wake the hind in covert slumbering, [...]

Loved was the voice that woo'd from Yarrow bowers
   Thy truant flight to that entrancing clime; [...]

Should her fair hand bestow the earliest bays,
   Although proud learning lift the venom'd eye,
Still shalt thou warble strains of other days, [...]

  Till those, who long have pass'd derisive by,
Shalt list to hear thy tones when newly strung.
       (Conclusion, ll. 1–4, 10–11, 19–21, 23–24)

Reading *Mador of the Moor* with a recognition of its historical and cultural contexts and with an acknowledgement of the importance of 'The Harper's Song', along with an awareness of Hogg's structural plan for the five cantos, not only raises the reader's appreciation of the artistic qualities of the poem, but also highlights the ways in which structure and theme, especially the theme of two conflicting world views, are deftly interconnected.

But the structure also brings into sharp focus another theme, the possibility of a new society in which all individuals receive recognition for their real worth. No analogue or antecedent has been discovered for the name of Mador. Hogg may have hoped to drive home the change in the character of the king by eliding 'made' and 'over' into Mador. Perhaps in using the name 'Mador' Hogg intends to emphasize that this is a new creature ('made o'er') who leaves the court to take up his new responsibilities. Because Ila Moore, not Mador, becomes the central figure in the poem, numerous issues which have particular relevance, not only to Hogg but to readers today, are raised. On the surface, elements of the poem may appear to be stereotypically patriarchal: a reduced and helpless woman, a callous nobleman, an enraged father, and a strong but conniving mother. But a closer reading tends to reveal more ambiguous gender roles. Without doubt Hogg constructs traditional worlds and employs stereotypical characters in *Mador of the Moor*, but he also raises the poem to a new level by questioning those worlds and stereotypes. In fact, he appears to be outlining the parameters of a brave new world. Ila survives because she is independent, dominating, and strong. In fact, she dominates the narrative's action and the poem's structure, and is much more interesting than the title character. And Kincraigy, a man struggling to understand his daughter, spans several value systems, as he takes tentative steps toward a redefinition of the role of father. The masculine world of the opening canto is completely undercut in the final canto when Mador abjures his court for the country. Whether he ever really belonged to the world of hunting and preying remains an unresolved question. Perhaps he too is a product of the patriarchal hegemony, yet desperately wants and needs to find a way to be a different kind of man. Granting these premises, perhaps then the narrator's telling comment at Canto II l. 171 carries multiple meanings:

When beauty gives command, all mankind must obey.

Notes

1. See Hogg's 'Memoir of the Author's Life' and 'Reminiscences of Former Days', in the *Altrive Tales* volume of the Stirling / South Carolina Research Edition of the Collected Works of James Hogg (hereafter S/SC Edition): Hogg, *Altrive Tales*, ed. by Gillian Hughes (S/SC, 2003), 11–78 (p. 34)–hereafter is cited in the text as 'Memoir'. For valuable biographical details and for information about the publication history of *Mador of the Moor*, I am indebted to the careful scholarly research of Gillian Hughes, Janette Currie, and Suzanne Gilbert.

2. For Gillian Hughes's argument, see Hogg, *Altrive Tales*, ed. Hughes, pp. 234–35.

3. For this and subsequent references to letters by Hogg, see *The Collected Letters of James Hogg: Volume 1 1800–1819*, ed. by Gillian Hughes and others (S/SC, 2004) (hereafter *Letters 1*). Hogg's letters are arranged chronologically in this edition, and can be readily traced in it by their date. For 'Mrs. Grant', see below at p. lvi note 25.

4. Quoted in *Letters 1* in the editorial commentary on Hogg's letter to John Murray of 1 March 1816.

5. On 29 March 1816 Blackwood writes to Murray: 'I am going on with the printing of "Mador of the Moor" Mr Hogg's new poem. I have made no bargain at all with him yet, but when I do so I will write you, and you can then take a share or not as you may like best' (quoted in *Letters 1* in the editorial commentary on Hogg's letter to William Blackwood of 11 April 1816).

6. See Hogg, *Altrive Tales*, ed. Hughes, p. 234.

7. For Blackwood's letter to Murray of 27 April 1816 see John Murray Archive, Blackwood Box 2. Blackwood's letter to Murray of 6/7 June 1816 is cited in *Letters 1* in the annotation for Hogg's letter to Anne Bald of 1 June 1816.

8. John Murray Archive, *Books Printed for John Murray* [...] *May 1817*, p. 9.

9. The following reviews are known: *Scots Magazine*, 78 (June 1816),

448–51; *New Monthly Magazine*, 5 (June 1816), 444–45; *Champion*, (9 June 1816), 181–82; *Critical Review*, 5th series 4 (August 1816), 130–43; *Literary Panorama*, n.s. 4 (August 1816), 731–40; *British Lady's Magazine*, 4 (October 1816), 251–55; *Monthly Review*, 81 (December 1816), 438–40; *British Critic*, n.s. 7 (January 1817), 97–100; *Eclectic Review*, 2nd series 7 (February 1817), 174–79; *Anti-Jacobin Review*, 52 (June 1817), 328–35.

10. For a helpful discussion by Peter Garside of Hogg's 'ancient stile', see Hogg, *A Queer Book*, ed. by P. D. Garside (S/SC, 1995), pp. xv–xvi.
11. For example, see Hogg's letter to William Blackwood of 28 March [1828] (National Library of Scotland, MS 4021, fols 277–78).
12. *Quarterly Review*, 44 (1831), 82.
13. James Hogg, *Memoir of the Author's Life; and, Familiar Anecdotes of Sir Walter Scott*, ed. by Douglas S. Mack (New York: Barnes and Noble, 1972), p. ix.
14. James Hogg, *The Queen's Wake*, ed. by Douglas S. Mack (S/SC, 2004), pp. 62–63. Several of the bards of *The Queen's Wake* are recognisable portraits of Scottish poets of Hogg's own day, and in a surviving copy of the fifth edition of the poem (1819), Hogg has provided manuscript annotations which identify the poets involved. Here he describes the Tenth Bard as 'The author James Hogg'. This copy, now owned by Douglas S. Mack, is described in Alan Grant, 'A Presentation Copy of *The Queen's Wake*', *Newsletter of the James Hogg Society*, 8 (1989), 21–22.
15. James Hogg, *The Pilgrims of the Sun* (Edinburgh: Blackwood; London, Murray, 1815), p. 121.
16. All references to the text of *Mador of the Moor* relate to the present edition.
17. Raphael Holinshed, *The Scottish Chronicle*, 2 vols (Arbroath: J. Findlay, 1805), II, 29–43. It appears that Hogg was familiar with this edition. He quotes from it in *The Queen's Wake*: see S/SC edition, p. 178. See also Hogg, *Queen Hynde*, ed. by Suzanne Gilbert and Douglas S. Mack (S/SC, 1998), p. 238.
18. See Walter Scott, *Tales of a Grandfather [First Series]*, 3 vols (Edinburgh: Cadell; London: Simpkin and Marshall; Dublin: Cumming, 1828), III, 56–62.
19. See James Hogg, *The Jacobite Relics of Scotland: Second Series*, ed. by Murray G. H. Pittock (S/SC, 2003), pp. 509–12. In his notes to this edition, Pittock carefully delineates the sources of this legend in popular ballads and songs. I am indebted to him for the substance and form of these insights. See also Appendix II in the present edition.
20. Walter Scott, *The Lady of the Lake* (Edinburgh: Ballantyne; London: Longman, 1810). Hereafter cited in the text as *Lady*.
21. 'Malise's Journey to the Trossacks, with a romantic Highland tale': see James Hogg, *The Spy*, ed. by Gillian Hughes (S/SC, 2000), 397–402 (p. 397). Hereafter cited in the text as *The Spy*. Hogg's epigraph for 'Malise's Journey' comes from Canto I, division XII, ll. 23–24 of *The Lady of the Lake*.

22. James Hogg, *Anecdotes of Scott*, ed. by Jill Rubenstein (S/SC, 1999), p. 43. Hereafter cited in the text as *Anecdotes*.

23. Alexander Pope, *The Rape of the Lock and Other Poems*, ed. by Geoffrey Tillotson (London: Methuen, 1940), p. 154. Hereafter cited in the text as *Rape*.

24. Hogg's admiration for Pope is expressed in his two 'Letters on Poetry', published in the May 1805 and January 1806 numbers of the *Scots Magazine*: 67 (May 1805), 352–53; 68 (January 1806), 17–18. In the first letter, Hogg writes, 'I cannot now think of a better rule, nor a shorter one, than that line of Mr Pope's, in which he describes true wit' (p. 353).

25. Lord Byron, *The Complete Poetical Works*, ed. by Jerome J. McGann, 7 vols (Oxford: Clarendon Press, 1980–93), III, 149.

26. Kurt Wittig, *The Scottish Tradition in Literature* (Edinburgh: Oliver and Boyd, 1958), p. 117.

27. *The Poems of James VI of Scotland*, ed. by James Craigie (Edinburgh: Blackwood, 1958), p. xxvi.

28. Thomas Hudson, *Historie of Judith*, ed. by James Craigie (Edinburgh: Blackwood, 1941), p. xcviii.

29. Mary Jane Scott, 'James Thomson and the Anglo-Scots', in *The History of Scottish Literature: Volume 2 1660–1800* (Aberdeen: Aberdeen University Press, 1987), p. 81.

30. See Wittig, p. 155.

31. Mary Jane Scott, p. 81.

32. David Hill Radcliffe, 'Crossing Borders: The Untutored Genius as Spenserian Poet', *John Clare Society Journal*, 22 (2003), 51–67 (p. 51).

33. Radcliffe, p. 53.

34. Jonathan Rose, *The Intellectual Life of the British Working Classes* (New Haven: Yale University Press, 2001), p. 115.

35. *The Norton Anthology of English Literature*, ed. by Meyer Abrams and others, 2 vols (New York: Norton, 1993), I, 2450.

James Hogg's Literary Friendships with John Grieve and Eliza Izett

Janette Currie

In his recent Introduction to *The Queen's Wake* (S/SC, 2004), Douglas S. Mack describes how patronage played an important part in the development of Hogg's literary career. Mack writes:

> Through his friendship with Scott, Hogg had links with the world of the literary superstars of Edinburgh's intellectual and social elite. However, the failed Dumfriesshire farmer's life in the early 1810s was centred on a different Edinburgh, an Edinburgh with which he was in lively contact through *The Spy* and the Forum.[1]

This 'different Edinburgh' included people such as Eliza Izett, to whom, as James Barcus notes in the Introduction to the present volume, Hogg gave the credit for his beginning to write *Mador of the Moor*, and also John Grieve, to whom this poem 'descriptive of the Tay' is dedicated. In the early years of Hogg's literary career both were clearly significant to his development as a writer. Indeed, Hogg claims in his dedication 'To Mr. John Grieve', 'That never song of mine had seen the day, | But for thy friendship and unchanged regard' (ll. 8–10).

Mack quotes at length from Susan Manning's review of Gillian Hughes's edition of *The Spy* (S/SC, 2000), where Manning discusses how the volume's 'Notes on Contributors' depict also the social circles of the 'different Edinburgh' in which Hogg moved in the 1810s. Manning found particular value in Hughes's depiction of the

> fascinating, dense alternative if not counter culture flourishing in early nineteenth-century Edinburgh. This is not a world of lairds, lawyers and aristocrats, the visible face of Scotland's official literary landscape in the Regency period, where Scott, Jeffrey, Mackenzie and Wilson were the legislators and Hogg would always, as an outsider, be an easy target. Here instead are professionals: printers, schoolteachers, physicians, working farmers. And also women, not only as subjects of adoration or satire, but also as authors, contributors in their own right to social debate.[2]

John Grieve and Eliza Izett were part of this 'alternative if not counter culture'. Frequently during the 1810s Hogg sought their advice on literary and personal matters, and included them in discussions of his work-in-progress. Understanding Hogg's friendships with Grieve and Izett reveals much previously invisible about the cultural context of Hogg's work of the period that produced poems such as *Mador of the Moor*. As it attempts to reveal a little more of Scotland's 'unofficial literary landscape', this essay builds on the recent research of Gillian Hughes and others such as Richard D. Jackson.[3]

Hogg claimed in his 'Memoir of the Author's Life' to have 'been acquainted' with Grieve 'from our youth', and it may be that they met as young men in Ettrick.[4] Grieve was born in Dunfermline, on 12 September 1781, but in early childhood his family moved to Cacrabank, in the Ettrick Valley. Richard D. Jackson notes that Grieve's 'mother, Jane or Jean Ballantyne, was the daughter of George Ballantyne, the tenant of Craig, in the parish of Yarrow. Walter Grieve was the uncle of William Laidlaw, Sir Walter Scott's factor'.[5] Following an early appointment as clerk to Mr Virtue, a wood-merchant in Alloa, and a situation in a bank in Greenock, from around 1802 Grieve was entered into partnership with Francis Bald, a merchant in Alloa. During his time in Alloa Grieve formed a friendship with another merchant, Alexander Bald, and together the two men visited Hogg 'long prior to his public recognition as a poet.'[6] After Francis Bald's death, Grieve formed a partnership in 1804 with an Edinburgh hat-maker named Chalmers Izett, a man Hogg described as 'singular for his attention to and consequently success in business'.[7]

Elizabeth Izett (née Stewart) was born on 9 June 1774, 'to Mr James Stewart writter in Dowally and Jannet Hagart his Lawfull Spous', and was baptised four days later in the parish of Dowally in the County of Perth. Her family had lived in Dowally Parish for some time as her grandfather, John Stewart, is noted as holding the important responsibility of 'tacksman of the millin of Dowally'.[8] The 'tacksman' collected all rents and taxes on behalf of the local landowner or laird, in this case, the Duke of Atholl. The entry for Dowally in the *Statistical Account of Scotland* (1791–99) records: 'excepting the barony of Dalcapon, all the lands in the parish are thirled to the mill of Dowally', which means that John Stewart would have been paid a proportion of all of the grain ground at the mill.[9] In the spring of 1792, Elizabeth Stewart married Chalmers Izett in Dowally, and thereafter moved to Edinburgh.[10]

Hogg mentions visiting the Atholl valley in 'A Journey Through the Highlands of Scotland, in the Months of July and August 1802, in A Series of Letters to S—— W——, Esq.', published in the *Scots Magazine* (October and December 1802, and February, April, and May 1803). In the second part of 'Letter IV' (which appeared in May 1803), Hogg describes passing through the Atholl Valley and the people that he met there, and although he 'passed the hill called King's Seat, which riseth immediately from the river with a steep ascent to the top, and hath a very striking appearance', he never specifically mentions Elizabeth Stewart of Dowally, or the Izetts of Kinnaird.[11]

John Grieve accompanied Hogg on at least one of his many tours of the Scottish Highlands. In 'A Journey through the Highlands and Western Isles, in the Summer of 1804.— In a Series of Letters to a Friend, By the Ettrick Shepherd', Grieve is named interchangeably as 'Mr J.', 'Mr John' and 'Mr G.'. In the first letter, Hogg describes his companion:

Mr John [...] besides a good memory and judgement, had a mind extremely sensible to all the finer feelings: a taste for the sublime and beautiful, but rather too high-flavoured, to be generally good: enthusiastically fond of poetry and music, and no mean proficient in either: paid perhaps a little more deference to the opinions and temper of others than the former [William Laidlaw, who also accompanied them], but was ten times more impatient at being thwarted by contrary elements. From the habits of a town life, he had acquired ideas of the different degrees of mankind, and subordination of ranks, quite above what either Mr W. [William Laidlaw] or I had any conception of; and thought himself justly entitled to knock down every little d—d fellow or impertinent gipey of a girl, who did not answer a question or obey an order exactly to his mind, but withal possessed of an honest and generous heart.[12]

On this 1804 visit to the Highlands, Hogg and Grieve did not travel near to where the Izetts were in the process of building the new mansion-house of Kinnaird on land they had purchased in 1798. Once complete, around 1805, Kinnaird House became the Izetts' summer residence where they entertained visitors from the city, including Hogg and Grieve. In the spring of 1810 they moved permanently to Kinnaird House, apparently due to Mrs Izett's 'delicate constitution'.[13] Kinnaird House is described in an advertisement for a 'Beautiful Estate in Perthshire' in the *Perthshire Courier* of 14 June 1812:

> The mansion-house was built within these seven years, and is finished in a very superior style; it contains three public rooms (the drawing-room 24 feet by 18), eight bedrooms, besides kitchen, servant's rooms, water-closets, &c. [...] The garden contains nearly two English acres, all enclosed within a stone wall about 12 feet high. The trees are all in full bearing, both in the orchards and garden. [...] The river Tay runs through the estate, affording several excellent draughts, for upwards of a mile, for salmon and trout; and the estate abounds with game of all sorts. There are several miles of walks, cut along the bank of the river and through the woods, commanding many beautiful and romantic views. In short, such a desirable property as this is seldom to be met with, and of which no adequate description can be given in an advertisement.

The estate does not appear to have been sold at this time as Chalmers Izett continued to conduct his Edinburgh business from here, as well as becoming involved in local affairs; for example *Morrison's Perth and Perthshire Register for 1815* names him as a Commissioner of Supply and one of the Curators of the McIntosh Library. The Izetts had an 'open house' policy at Kinnaird House, where they entertained visitors on a regular basis. John Wilson stayed for a week in the summer of 1815 while on a walking tour of the Highlands with his wife. In September of that year, Wilson wrote to Hogg about his tour: 'Mrs Wilson and I walked 350 miles in the Highlands, between the 5th of July and the 26th of August [...] We stayed seven days at Mrs. Izett's, at Kinnaird, and were most kindly received. Mrs. Izett is a great ally of yours, and is a fine creature'.[14] Hogg often visited Kinnaird House where he had access to Mrs Izett's private library. In his letter to Eliza Izett of 11 February 1814, he describes the library as 'the neat collection up stairs which has erst been free to me'.[15] Around 1822 the Izetts sold Kinnaird House and moved to Blairgowrie in Perthshire, to a house named 'Altamont'. It is not recorded if Hogg visited them there.[16]

In 1808, Hogg was in financial straits. His farming venture at Locherben in Dumfriesshire—paid for with his earnings from his two published volumes of the previous year, *The Mountain Bard* and *The Shepherd's Guide: Being a Practical Treatise on the Diseases of Sheep* (1807), had failed. Around this time Chalmers Izett put a business proposition to Hogg, most probably the tenancy of one of the farms

at Kinnaird.[17] It was an offer that Hogg graciously refused. He told
Mrs Izett in his letter of 23 July 1808 'I certainly will never forget
his generous offer', and he also writes:

> We must however think no more of it, for a man who has
> not stock sufficient to make the most of a farm, and to enable
> him to carry his views into execution is only an encumbrance
> on his Land-lord which I would certainly be on Mr. Izet. Be-
> sides I have a fault in farming which I have but lately discov-
> ered: Servants do not stand in sufficient awe of me. Not that
> they ever refuse my orders which they always do with the
> greatest alacrity but often neglect their duty with impunity not
> being in the least afraid of my censure.

At this time, Grieve also offered his support to Hogg. In a letter to
Walter Scott of 28 July 1809, Hogg told Scott:

> Mr. Grieve the hatter has been a true and a liberal [friend] to
> me. He is some way or another convinced of my superior
> merit as a *poet* and nothing else influences him in the least: he
> has supplied me constantly with newspapers clothes, shoes,
> hats, and pocket money whenever he knew I wanted it.

Along with a fellow Ettrick-man named Henry Scott, another part-
ner in the Izett hatter's business, Grieve continued to offer his mate-
rial and financial support when Hogg moved to Edinburgh in Febru-
ary 1810.[18] Hogg noted their benevolence in his 'Memoir of the
Author's Life':

> During the first six months that I resided in Edinburgh I lived
> with him [Grieve], and his partner, Mr. Scott, who, on a longer
> acquaintance, became as firmly attached to me as Mr. Grieve;
> and, I believe, as much so as to any other man alive. We three
> have had many very happy evenings together; we indeed were
> seldom separate when it was possible to meet. They suffered
> me to want for nothing, either in money or clothes; and I did
> not even need to ask these. Mr. Grieve was always the first to
> notice my wants, and prevent them. In short, they would not
> suffer me to be obliged to any one but themselves for the
> value of a farthing; and without this sure support I could never
> have fought my way in Edinburgh. I was fairly starved into it,
> and if it had not been for Messrs. Grieve and Scott, would, in
> a very short time, have been starved out of it again. (p. 27)

Grieve eventually found lodgings for Hogg close to Grieve and

Scott's hat-making business on the North Bridge. His rooms were in an alley-way called Gabriel's Road. This local short-cut was often used by students of Edinburgh University as it led from the east side of Saint Andrew's Square and came out at the far end of Princes Street directly opposite to the North Bridge.[19]

As Hogg noted in his biographical description in 'A Journey through the Highlands and Western Isles', Grieve was a minor poet. Along with Alexander Bald, Grieve had several poems (signed, 'G., Banks of Etterick') published in the short-lived Edinburgh periodical *The North British Magazine and Review*, edited by Andrew Mercer. In 1810 both Grieve and the Izetts were involved in the preparation and selection of material for Hogg's song-collection entitled *The Forest Minstrel* (Edinburgh: Constable; London: Constable, Hunter, Park and Hunter, 1810). Peter Garside has written of Hogg's changing social status at this time:

> With his rise to the status of tenant farmer, partly on the proceeds of the *Mountain Bard*, Hogg's social horizons expanded, as through trips to Edinburgh he became acquainted with James Gray and with the feminine social circle of Eliza Izett, the wife of John Grieve's partner in trade, and in the process with the more polite song scene of the genteel middle-class drawing room. It is important to bear in mind that it was this social world of Gray and Grieve which provided Hogg's main support system in the build-up to *The Forest Minstrel*.[20]

Some of Grieve's early poems were republished in *The Forest Minstrel*, denoted by the letter 'C. Anonymous', alongside contributions by Hogg and others. For example, Grieve's poem 'To Caroline' was published with the revised title 'Caroline', on p. 57 of *The Forest Minstrel*.[21] In a letter of 11 December 1808 to Mrs Izett, Hogg mentions two songs, one of which is certainly connected with *The Forest Minstrel*:

> My kindest respects to Mr. Izet and the amiable Miss Forest; the next time I come to Edin I will bring verses with me to the tunes of Lord Eglingtons auld man and the other gaelic air but I have finished no small piece nor indeed any piece at all since I saw you.[22]

Hogg later noted that 'Miss C.[halmers] Forrest', Mr and Mrs Izett's niece, had performed his songs at the piano, and had set some of them to music.[23] In notes to his collection of *Songs, by the Ettrick Shepherd* (Edinburgh: Blackwood; London: Cadell, 1831), Hogg records that he had heard 'one young lady (Miss Forrest)' sing 'Caledonia', and that his song 'The Flower' was 'beautifully harmonized to a Gaelic air, by Miss C. Forest, in a single sheet', while 'The Moon was A-Waning' was 'the first song of mine I ever heard sung at the piano [...]. The song was first set to music and sung by Miss C. Forest, and has long been a favourite, and generally sung through a great portion of Scotland' (pp. 26, 242, and 253). The spring 1810 departure of the Izetts from Edinburgh to Kinnaird forms the subject of Hogg's song entitled 'The Bogles', clearly composed around this time.

> My bonny Eliza is fled frae the town,
> An' left her poor Jamie her loss to bemoan;
> To me 'tis a sad an' lamentable day;
> For the *bogles* have chas'd my Eliza away.
> The Lowlands may weep, and the Highlands may smile,
> In welcome to her that's the flower of our isle:
> It's all for thy honour, ambitious Tay,
> That the *bogles* have chas'd my Eliza away.   [...]
>
> I love her; I own it; I'll own it again;
> If I had two friends on the earth, she was ane;
> And now I can neither be cheerfu' nor gay,
> Since the bogles have chas'd my Eliza away.[24]

There is no doubt that Hogg's close friendships with John Grieve and Eliza Izett were a major influence on his writing career. In his 'Memoir of the Author's Life', Hogg describes Mrs Izett as a lady who

> had taken an early interest in my fortunes, which no circumstance has ever abated. I depended much on her advice and good taste; and had I attended more to her friendly remonstrances, it would have been much better for me.   (p. 34)

Aside from Hogg's deferential note in his 'Memoir', and the barest facts that the surviving Parish Records reveal, very little is known about Eliza Izett. She also corresponded with, and was interested in, the careers and lives of the Scottish novelist Mary Brunton, and the poet and author Anne Grant (of Laggan). Very little of Eliza Izett's correspondence with these two writers survives, and unfortunately, none of her side of the correspondence appears to be extant.[25]

For the first few years of the nineteenth century the Izetts lived at number six St John Street in Edinburgh, close to the Reverend Alexander and Mrs Brunton, who moved into number three late in

1803.[26] Alexander Brunton later noted their close friendship and recorded Mrs Izett's literary influence on his wife:

> The circumstance which, more than any other beyond the range of her own domestic intercourse, tended both to develope her intellect, and to establish her character, was an intimacy which she formed, soon after her removal to Edinburgh, with a lady in her immediate neighbourhood. They were indeed so near, that it was easy for them to be much together. They read together—worked together—and talked over, with confidential freedom, their opinions, from minuter points to the most important of all. [...] This intercourse continued for about six years, when it was interrupted by Mrs Izett's removal from Edinburgh. But it was not, and could not be suspended altogether; so far as letters could prolong it, it was continued to the last, by the only close and confidential correspondence, beyond the bounds of her own family, in which Mary ever engaged.[27]

The published correspondence reveals the extent of Mrs Izett's interest in Mary Brunton's writing, where Mrs Brunton discusses the composition of her novels and thanks Mrs Izett for her literary criticism of *Self-Control* (published in 1810, see *A Memoir of her Life*, pp. xlvii–l). In one of her letters dated 30 August 1810 Mary Brunton reprimands Mrs Izett on being 'far too sanguine in expecting strange good fortune to befal your friends. You not only look for roses in the wilderness, but roses without thorns' (*Memoir of her Life*, pp. xxxii–xxxviii, xxxvii). Mary Brunton died in 1819; however her husband, the Reverend Alexander Brunton, appears to have continued his friendship with the Izetts, as in 1841 he is one of the named executors of Chalmers Izett's will.[28]

Mrs Izett clearly expected 'strange good fortune to befal' her other literary friend, James Hogg. In what appears to be the first of his letters to her while she was on a summer visit to Kinnaird House, Hogg told Mrs Izett in his letter of 23 July 1808: 'I have always been very highly flattered Eliza by the attention paid to me by you [...] You are, like me, of a literary turn of mind, and even a considerable degree of similarity appears to prevail in our tastes and opinions'. With Mrs Izett and John Grieve, Hogg shared his plans for his literary career and projected work, frequently asking and taking note of their advice. In a letter from Hogg to Mrs Izett at Kinnaird dated October 1811, Hogg writes of his work as the editor of *The Spy* (published weekly in 1810 and 1811), and he tells her:

I hope I have pleased you in many of my papers both in prose and verse if I thought otherwise I should be very unhappy I have finished a highland tale lately and some smaller pieces which I would travel a good many miles to hear you read and learn your opinion of them.

In another letter to Mrs Izett of 23 March 1813, Hogg tells her of his publication plans for an edition of his tales, and also about a play he was currently writing:

As I take delight in nothing but literature I intend publishing two volumes of Scottish rural tales sometime this year I would be happy in having your advice which of those in the Spy I should select.[29] [...]

I have likewise begun to block out a *tragedy* [*The Hunting of Badlewe*, 1814] but remember both these are profound secrets and no other person must know of them save my own Eliza and our mutual friend Grieve. Have no fears about the latter for if it is not judged by my few friends even better than good it shall never appear.

And in his letter of 11 February 1814 he asks Mrs Izett's advice on his latest poem:

Some ladies of high distinguishment in letters have objected strongly to the title *Mador of the Moor* but Grieve who delights in such a dark mysterious title will by no means yeild to the giving it up I have been thinking of calling it *The Maiden of Tay* pray think upon it .[30]

Hogg's letter to Eliza Izett, of 14 December 1817, was written within 'two minutes' of receipt 'from my loved correspondent and her rainy habitation'. In this long letter, Hogg discloses his concerns for John Grieve's health:

Grieve I am sorry to say it is not well nor looking well a kind of feebleness about his loins is still increasing and he can now walk but little not even to the shop by himself at present, which I hope is only a temporary ailment [...].

He relates literary news of his latest works in progress:

I have sometimes been scribbling since I saw you but very seldom having for the most part been employed in farming fishing sailing &c. My Cottage tales in prose will be published in the spring two or four volumes as my friends shall advise after they have seen the first two

The Queen's Wake will not I fear be published this year as the subscriptions have come in but very slow and the work is expensive. We do not yet know of many above 200 and would like to have about 1000 before putting to press

And he declaims his admiration:

I have for a good long time now been very much chagrined at the whole of your sex and think them most unnaccountable creatures void of right feeling or consideration. In speaking of them however I always in my own mind make you an exception you are so disinterested so kind and affectionate and withal so refined and pure that though I could take you in my arms it would be as a sister whom I had not for a long while seen. I have now no hopes ever to live beside you or under your eye and in spite of my teeth your image passes away from my remembrance. But when ever it rises there it is a vision in which I delight

Overall, Hogg's correspondence with Eliza Izett gives just one side of their conversations, as her letters to him do not survive. Partial though it is, it reveals a further glimpse of his literary patron, and it allows us a tantalising glimpse into their genuinely warm, affectionate relationship.[31]

Hogg accorded Grieve the ultimate accolade of recognising him as the person who encouraged him to write *The Queen's Wake*, the major poem that arguably established Hogg's reputation as a poet.[32] Hogg claimed that following the success of Scott's and Byron's poetry, Grieve had the idea that Hogg should 'take the field once more as a poet, and try my fate with the others'. Hogg records in the 'Memoir of the Author's Life' that while he was writing *The Queen's Wake*, 'no one would either read it, or listen to my reading it, save Grieve, who assured me it would do' (p. 28). As a tribute to his friend, Hogg made the Fourteenth Bard in *The Queen's Wake* a portrait of Grieve. This Bard 'foremost came' in Night the Third, and he sings 'Mary Scott'. Hogg describes him as follows:

A youth he was of manly mold,
Gentle as lamb, as lion bold;
But his fair face, and forehead high,
Glowed with intrusive modesty.

'Twas said by bank of southland stream
Gilded his youth in soothing dream;
The harp he loved, and wont to stray
Far to the wilds and woods away,
And sing to brooks that gurgled bye
Of maiden's form and maiden's eye;
That, when this dream of youth was past,
Deep in the shade his harp he cast;
In busy life his cares beguiled;
His heart was true, and fortune smiled.[33]

On the day that *The Queen's Wake* was published in February 1813, it was Grieve who laid on a celebratory 'banquet' in Hogg's honour.[34] Mrs Izett, too, was delighted with Hogg's epic as is revealed in his letter to her of 23 March:

I am glad that you are pleased with the young Queen but not much flattered because I knew before that your friendship for the runagate author would insure that to a certain degree. It is more pleasant to hear the praises of strangers and the silence or rage of enemies. But indeed from what I know of the kindness of your heart I believe you have experienced more innate pleasure from the success of the work than I have done

From the early 1810s Grieve suffered from deterioration in his health that Charles Rogers described as 'a disorder of the spine'. His ill-health caused his early retirement from the hat business around 1818; nevertheless, his support and encouragement for Hogg continued.[35] R. P. Gillies notes that while in Edinburgh on business from Altrive Lake, his farm in the Yarrow Valley, Hogg often stayed at Grieve's house in Teviot-row, George Square, where 'he had the entire house to himself, with store of books and music, from the breakfast hour till dinner time'. Hogg's time in Grieve's house 'was about the happiest of his life, and he revolved numberless literary plans'.[36] Around this time, Hogg took an interest in the possibility that a house would be found on Scott's Abbotsford estate for Grieve's elderly father, a retired minister of the Reformed Presbyterian Church of Scotland. Referring to this plan (which in the event was never realised) Scott wrote to William Laidlaw: 'I cannot tell you how delighted I am with the account Hogg gives me of Mr Grieve.'[37]

As Hogg's literary career took off, he became more confident of publication success, and in his correspondence there is less notice of him seeking the opinion of his early literary advisers. Grieve moved out of Edinburgh to a cottage in the newly created suburban splendour of Newington, where he was joined in 1830 by Mr and Mrs Izett, who moved to a house in Blackett Place.[38] However, they continued to support and be interested in Hogg's literary career. In 1833, when Hogg quarrelled seriously with the publisher William Blackwood, John Grieve and the Izetts were involved in bringing them back together. On one of his business trips to Edinburgh, Hogg wrote to his wife, Margaret, that '[John] Wilson Grieve and the Izets are all engaged about it just now but as I have not been able to see any body I know not what is done'.[39] John Wilson explained to Hogg, 'I was induced to offer my services by my own sincere regard for you, and the wishes of Mrs. Izett and Mr. Grieve [...] I will merely mention to Mr. Grieve, who was desirous of having you and Mr. Blackwood and myself to dinner, that I wrote you'.[40] The result of their friendly interference was that Hogg resumed his communications with Blackwood.

John Grieve died five months after Hogg, on 4 April 1836, and Eliza Izett died on 16 October 1842. So ended the life-long literary friendships between the 'runagate author', his 'more than brother', and 'bonny Eliza'.

Notes

I would like to record my gratitude to Gillian Hughes who generously gave information in support of this essay, and also to Richard Jackson, for information supplied from his research in the National Archives of Scotland, Edinburgh, concerning Chalmers Izett's property transactions for Kinnaird House, and his will.

1. Hogg, *The Queen's Wake*, ed. by Douglas S. Mack (S/SC, 2004), p. xv.
2. See Susan Manning's review of Gillian Hughes's edition of *The Spy* (S/SC, 2000), in *Studies in Hogg and his World*, 11 (2000), 134–37 (p. 135).
3. Alongside of Hughes's edition of *The Spy*, see Hogg's *Altrive Tales*, ed. by Gillian Hughes (S/SC, 2003), and also the discussion of Hogg's early patrons John Grieve and Henry Scott in Richard D. Jackson, '*The Pirate* and "The Bonny Lass of Deloraine" ', in the *Scott Newsletter*, 40 (Summer 2002), 9–21, (pp. 16–19).
4. Hogg's 'Memoir of the Author's Life' in *Altrive Tales*, ed. Hughes, pp. 11–52 (p. 27). Subsequent references to the 'Memoir' are to this edition, and are given in the text.
5. Jackson, '*The Pirate* and "The Bonny Lass of Deloraine" ', p. 16.
6. See *Altrive Tales*, ed. Hughes, p. 221, note on 18c. Further information was derived from biographical notes for Hogg, Grieve, and Alexander Bald in *The Modern Scottish Minstrel*, ed. by Charles Rogers,

6 vols (Edinburgh, 1855–57), I, 1–80, III, 43–49, and V, 34–6 respectively. See also Jackson, '*The Pirate* and "The Bonny Lass of Deloraine" ', especially pp. 16–19. Hogg was still in contact with Alexander Bald in November 1813, when he wrote to him about *Mador of the Moor*, his latest work-in-progress: see *Altrive Tales*, ed. Hughes, p. 234, note on 34c.

7. In this essay Hogg's letters are quoted from *The Letters of James Hogg: Volume 1 1800–1819*, ed. by Gillian Hughes (S/SC, 2004) (hereafter *Letters 1*). In the S/SC edition Hogg's letters are arranged in chronological order, and can therefore be readily traced by their dates: full page references have therefore not been given. The comment quoted here appears in a letter which seems to be the first from Hogg to Eliza Izett. It was sent to 'Mrs C Izet Kinnaird Dunkeld', from Hogg at Locherben, his Dumfriesshire farm, on 23 July 1808. Further biographical details about Chalmers Izett can be found in *Letters 1*, pp. 457–60.

8. *Old Parish Register of Dowally*, 14 December 1771, and 13 June 1774: see *OPR* m/f 344/01.

9. *The Statistical Account of Scotland 1791–1799*, ed. by Sir John Sinclair, 20 vols (Wakefield: EP Publishing, 1975–83), XII: North and West Perthshire (1977), p. 382.

10. *Old Parish Register of Proclamations of Banns & Marriages for Dowally*, 14 and 15 April 1792: see *OPR* m/f 344/01. I am grateful to the curator of the Atholl Muniments at Blair Castle, for confirming this information about the Stewarts of Dowally.

11. For 'Letter IV' see the *Scots Magazine*, 65 (1803), 251–54 and 312–14. The extract quoted appears at p. 312.

12. Hogg's 'Journey through the Highlands and Western Isles' was serialised in the *Scots Magazine*, 70 (1808), in the numbers for June (423–26); August (569–72); September (672–74); October (735–38); November (809–11) and December (889–92): the extract quoted comes from the June 1808 number at pp. 423–24. I am grateful to Hans de Groot, who is currently editing the S/SC volume devoted to Hogg's *Highland Journeys*, for information on Dowally and for confirming that John Grieve accompanied Hogg on this tour.

13. Mentioned by Hogg in his letter of 23 July 1808: see also the *Edinburgh Weekly Journal*, 27 December 1809, where an advertisement signals Chalmers Izett's withdrawl from the hatter business (information from Richard Jackson).

14. Mary Gordon, '*Christopher North': A Memoir of John Wilson*, 2 vols (Edinburgh: Edmonston and Douglas, 1862), I, 197–98.

15. See Introduction, p. xxxix.

16. Information on the Izetts' legal transactions for Kinnaird House and Altamont can be found in the National Archives of Scotland (hereafter NAS), *Registers of Sasines for Perthshire*. See, in particular, 1781–1820 no. 4216 and 1821–30 no. 1887.

17. See Hogg's letter to Scott of 26 September 1808.

18. See Hughes's note 27(b) on p. 228 of her edition of Hogg, *The Spy*

(S/SC, 2000) for further biographical information on Henry Scott.

19. Further information on early nineteenth-century Edinburgh can be found in Mary Cosh, *Edinburgh: The Golden Age* (Edinburgh: John Donald, 2003). See also Stuart Harris, *The Place Names of Edinburgh* (Edinburgh: Gordon Wright Publishing, 1996), p. 282.

20. Peter Garside, 'Editing *The Forest Minstrel*: The Case of "By a Bush" ', *Studies in Hogg and his World*, 13 (2002), 72–94 (p. 79).

21. The poem first appeared in the *North British Magazine and Review*, 1 (1804), 240–42. No other volumes were published.

22. This letter is quoted in Garside, 'Editing *The Forest Minstrel*', (p. 87, note 33). Garside notes: 'the verses alluded to are "Lord Eglinton's auld Man" and (most probably) "The Moon was a-waning" (*Forest Minstrel*, pp. 33–34; 9–10), neither of which has a known publication history before the 1810 collection' (p. 87).

23. The *Old Parish Register of Tolbooth Kirk Parish*, Edinburgh of March 1790 records that 'James Forrest, merchant and Helen Izett his spouse' baptised their daughter, 'Chalmers' who was born on the 3 March 1790: see *OPR* m/film 658–1/38. As Chalmers Izett was present on the occasion and recorded as an official 'Witness', Helen Izett was presumably his sister.

24. James Hogg and others, *The Forest Minstrel: A Selection of Songs* (Edinburgh: Constable, 1810), pp. 87–88.

25. Anne Grant (1755–1838) was a minor poet who published a volume of poems in 1802. She moved to Edinburgh around 1810, although it is not recorded when she first met Hogg or Eliza Izett. She appears as one of 'The Scottish Muses' in Hogg's satirical essay on the Edinburgh literary scene of that name that he published in his literary newspaper, *The Spy* (1810–11), where she is described as 'rather a hard featured, Highland-looking maid, from the Braes of Badenoch, who had more of the matron appearance than the rest, and was characterized by gravity and decorum; she muttered much about the progress of the Celtic fragments from their native Gaelic, to their modern English dress': see *The Spy*, ed. Hughes (S/SC, 2000), p. 98 and also Hughes's note on p. 586. Anne Grant's letters contain snippets of gossip and news from Edinburgh to 'Mrs Izett, Kinnaird, Dunkeld', as well as personal messages concerning Mrs Grant's family: see *Memoir and Correspondence of Mrs Grant of Laggan*, ed. by J. P. Grant, 3 vols (London, 1844), ii, 299–300, 317–20; iii, 200–01, 225–26, 228–29, 250–53, 267–69, 285–87, 302–04, and 314–16.

26. See Mary McKerrow, *Mary Brunton: The Forgotten Scottish Novelist*, foreword by Fay Weldon (Kirkwall: *The Orcadian*, 2001), p. 79. McKerrow mistakenly refers to Mrs Izett as 'an untitled Yorkshire woman' (p. 79).

27. *Emmeline, with Some Other Pieces, by Mary Brunton, to which is prefixed, A Memoir of her Life; including some extracts from her correspondence* (Edinburgh: Manners & Miller; London: Murray, 1819), pp. xvi–xvii.

28. Chalmers Izett died on 17 April 1840: see NAS, SC 70/1/60, pp. 580–83.

29. These eventually formed the basis for *The Brownie of Bodsbeck and Other Tales*, 2 vols (Edinburgh: Blackwood; London: Murray, 1818) and *Winter Evening Tales*, 2 vols (Edinburgh: Oliver & Boyd; London: Whittaker, 1820).
30. See the Introduction, p. xiii.
31. Ten extant letters from Hogg to Eliza Izett can be found in *Letters 1*.
32. For further information on Grieve's part in the poem that brought Hogg the literary fame he so eagerly sought, see Mack's Introduction to Hogg, *The Queen's Wake* (S/SC, 2004).
33. See 'Night the Third', ll. 96–109 in *The Queen's Wake*, ed. Mack (S/SC, 2004).
34. David Groves, *James Hogg: The Growth of a Writer* (Edinburgh: Scottish Academic Press, 1988), p. 37.
35. Rogers notes that Alexander Bald supplied 'a number of particulars' for his biographical note for John Grieve (v, 34).
36. *Memoirs of a Literary Veteran*, 3 vols (London, 1851), II, 241–42. Richard Jackson has suggested that there were probably downs as well as ups during the long period of their relationship. His suggestion is borne out in the first (and only published) volume of Alan Lang Strout's *Life and Letters of James Hogg the Ettrick Shepherd*, where Strout points out that in his denunciatory *Letter to a Friend in London* in 1821, Hogg's former publisher, George Goldie, 'triumphantly declares that even John Grieve expostulated with Hogg' at this time (Lubbock, Texas, 1946), pp. 88–90. See also Grieve's correspondence with George Boyd in the Oliver and Boyd Archives, NLS, Acc. 5000 / 190–92.
37. See John Gibson Lockhart, *Memoirs of the Life of Sir Walter Scott, Bart.*, 7 vols (Edinburgh: Cadell; London: Murray and Whittaker, 1837–38) IV, 131.
38. *Altrive Tales*, ed. Hughes, p. 234, note on 34 (b).
39. Norah Parr, *James Hogg at Home* (Dollar: Mack, 1980), p. 115.
40. Gordon, *'Christopher North'*, II, 217–219 (p. 218).

MADOR OF THE MOOR;

A POEM.

BY JAMES HOGG,

AUTHOR OF THE QUEEN'S WAKE, &C.

Wild mirth of the desart! fit pastime for Kings,
Which still the rude Bard in his solitude sings.
WILSON.

EDINBURGH:

PRINTED FOR WILLIAM BLACKWOOD:

AND JOHN MURRAY, ALBEMARLE-STREET, LONDON.

1816.

To
Mr John Grieve

IF I knew man on earth that loved me more,
Or more approved my wayward minstrelsy,
Beshrew my pen, so prone to rhyming lore,
If it should dedicate this Book to thee:
But when I think of all thy truth to me,
And love, though sorely tried, that ne'er gave way,
At once all thoughts of loftier patron flee.
Slight is the gift; for, need I blush to say,
That never song of mine had seen the day,
But for thy friendship and unchanged regard?
To thee I owe them—How shall I repay
My more than brother!—all thy poor reward
Is this, thy favourite lay, of thy too favour'd Bard.

Advertisement

THE following Poem is partly founded on an incident recorded in the Scottish annals of the 14th century. The alteration in the lady's name, which was Elizabeth Moore, was necessary on account of the rythm.

Mador of the Moor

Introduction

Introduction

1.

THOU Queen of Caledonia's mountain floods,
   Theme of a thousand gifted Bards of yore,
Majestic wanderer of the wilds and woods,
   That lovest to circle cliff and mountain hoar,
   And with the winds to mix thy kindred roar,   5
Startling the shepherd of the Grampian glen!
   Rich are the vales that bound thy eastern shore,
And fair thy upland dales to human ken;
But scarcely are thy springs known to the sons of men.

2.

O that some spirit at the midnight noon   10
   Aloft would bear me, middle space, to see
Thy thousand branches gleaming to the moon,
   By shadowy hill, gray rock, and fairy lea;
   Thy gleesome elves disporting merrily
In glimmering circles by the lonely dell,   15
   Or by the sacred fount, or haunted tree,
Where bow'd the saint, as hoary legends tell,
And Superstition's last, wild, thrilling visions dwell!

3.

To Fancy's eye the ample scene is spread,
   The yellow moon-beam sleeps on hills of dew,   20
On many an everlasting pyramid
   That bathes its gray head in celestial blue.
   These o'er thy cradle stand the guardians true,
Th' eternal bulwarks of the land and thee,
   And evermore thy lullaby renew   25
To howling winds and storms that o'er thee flee:
All hail, ye battlements of ancient liberty!

4.

There the dark raven builds his dreary home;
  The eagle o'er his eyrie raves aloud;
The brindled fox around thee loves to roam,   30
  And ptarmigans, the inmates of the cloud;
  And when the summer flings her dappled shroud
O'er reddening moors, and wilds of soften'd gray,
  The youthful swain, unfashion'd, unendow'd,
The brocket and the lamb may round thee play: 35
These thy first guests alone, thou fair, majestic Tay!

5.

But bear me, Spirit of the gifted eye,
  Far on thy pinions eastward to the main,
O'er garish glens and straths of every dye,
  Where oxen low and waves the yellow grain;   40
  Where beetling cliffs o'erhang the belted plain
In spiral forms, fantastic, wild, and riven;
  Where swell the woodland choir and maiden's strain,
As forests bend unto the breeze of even,
And in the flood beneath wave o'er a downward heaven.   45

6.

Then hold thy vision'd course along the skies,
  O'er fertile vallies bounded by the sea,
Girdled by silver baldrick, which now vies
  In broadness with the ocean's majesty;
  Where pleasure smiles and laughing luxury,   50
And traffic bustles out the live-long day;
Where brazen keels before the billows flee—
  Is that the murmuring rill of mountain gray?
Is that imperial flood the wilder'd Grampian Tay?

7.

Far on thy fringed borders, west away,   55
  Queen of green Albyn's rivers, let me roam,
And mark thy graceful windings as I stray
  When drowsy day-light seeks her curtain'd dome.
  Fain would a weary wanderer from his home,
The wayward Minstrel of a southland dale,   60
  Sing of thy mountain birth, thy billowy tomb,
And legends old that linger in thy vale;
To friendship, and to thee, is due the simple tale.

8.

Old Caledonia! pathway of the storm
  That o'er thy wilds resistless sweeps along,   65
Though clouds and snows thy sterile hills deform,
  Thou art the land of freedom and of song!
  Land of the eagle fancy, wild and strong!
Land of the loyal heart and valiant arm!
  Though southern pride and luxury may wrong   70
Thy mountain honours, still my heart shall warm
At thy unquestion'd weir, and songs of magic charm.

9.

O, I might tell where ancient cities stood!
  And I might sing of battles lost and won;
Of royal obsequies, and halls of blood;   75
  And daring deeds by dauntless warrior done.
  Since Scotland's crimson page was first begun,
Tay was the scene of actions great and high;
  But aye when from the echoing hills I run,
My froward harp refuses to comply;—   80
The nursling of the wild, the Mountain Bard am I.

10.

I cannot sing of Longcarty and Hay,
  Nor long on deeds of death and danger dwell;
Of old Dunsinnan towers, or Birnam gray,
  Where Canmore battled and the Villain fell.   85
  But list! I will an ancient story tell,
A tale of meikle woe and mystery,
  Of sore mishaps that an Old Sire befel,
Wise Dame, and Minstrel of full high degree,
And visions of dismay, unfitting man to see.   90

11.

And thou shalt hear of Maid, whose melting eye
  Spoke to the heart what tongue could never say—
A maid right gentle, frolicsome, and sly,
  And blyth as lambkin on a morn of May;
  Whose auburn locks, when waving to the day,   95
And lightsome form of sweet simplicity,
  Stole many a fond unweeting heart away,
And held those hearts in pleasing slavery.
Woe that such flower should e'er by lover blighted be!

12.

But ween not thou that Nature's simple Bard   100
   Can e'er unblemish'd character define;
True to his faithful monitor's award,
   He paints her glories only as they shine.
   Of men all pure, and maidens all divine,
Expect not thou his wild-wood lay to be;   105
   But those whose virtues and defects combine,
Such as in erring man we daily see—
The child of failings born, and scathed humanity.

Mador of the Moor

Canto First

The Hunting

Argument

God prosper long our noble king,
* Our lives and safeties all!*
A woeful hunting once there did
* In Chevy Chace befall:*
To drive the deer with hound and horn
* Earl Percy took his way;*
The child may rue that is unborn
* The hunting of that day!*

Mador of the Moor

Canto First

The Hunting

1.

HASTE, ranger, to the Athol mountains blue!
  Unleash the hounds, and let the bugles sing!
The thousand traces in the morning dew,
  The bounding deer, the black-cock on the wing,
  Bespeak the rout of Scotland's gallant king;
The bearded rock shouts to the desart hoar;
  Haste, ranger!—all the mountain echoes ring,
From cairn of Bruar to the dark Glen-More,
The forest's in a howl, and all is wild uproar!

2.

O many a gallant hart that time was slain!
  And many a roe-buck founder'd in the glen!
The gor-cock beat the shivering winds in vain;
  The antler'd rover sought his widow'd den;
  Even birds that ne'er had seen the forms of men,
But roosted careless on the desart doone,
  An easy mark to ruthless archer's ken!
No more they whirr and crow at dawning boon,
Far on their grizzled heights, contiguous to the moon!

3.

Where'er the chace to dell or valley near'd,
  There for the royal train the feast was laid;
 There was the monarch's light pavilion rear'd;
  There flow'd the wine, and much in glee was said
  Of lady's form, and blooming mountain maid;
And many a fair was toasted to the brim:
  But knight and squire a languishing betray'd
When *one* was named, whose eye made diamonds dim!
The King look'd sad and sigh'd! no sleep that night for him!

5

10

15

20

25

4.

The morning rose, but scarce they could discern
　　When Night gave in her sceptre to the day,
The clouds of heaven were moor'd so dark and dern,　　30
　　And wrapt the forest in a shroud of gray.
　　Man, horse, and hound, in listless languor lay,
For the wet rack traversed the mountain's brow;
　　But, long ere night, the Monarch stole away;
His courtiers search'd, and raised the loud halloo,　　35
But well they knew their man, and made not much ado.

5.

Another day came on, another still,
　　And aye the clouds their drizzly treasures shed;
The pitchy mist hung moveless on the hill,
　　And hooded every pine-tree's reverend head:　　40
　　The heavens seem'd sleeping on their mountain bed,
The straggling roes mistimed their noontide den,
　　And stray'd the forest, belling for the dead,
Started at every rustle–paused, and then
Sniff'd, whistling in the wind, and bounded to the glen.　　45

6.

The King was lost, and much conjecture past.
　　At length the morning rose in lightsome blue,
Far to the west her pinken veil she cast;
　　Up rose the fringed sun, and softly threw
　　A golden tint along the moorland dew:　　50
The mist had sought the winding vales, and lay
　　A slumbering ocean of the softest hue,
Where mimic rainbows bent in every bay,
And thousand islets smiled amid the watery way.

7.

The steeps of proud Ben-Glow the nobles scaled,　　55
　　For there they heard their Monarch's bugle yell;
First on the height, the beauteous morn he hail'd,
　　And rested, wondering, on the heather bell.
　　The amber blaze that tipt the moor and fell,
The fleecy clouds that roll'd afar below,　　60
　　The hounds' impatient whine, the bugle's swell,
Raised in his breast a more than wonted glow.
The nobles found him pleased, nor farther strove to know.

8.

The driver circle narrow'd on the heath,
   Close, and more close, the deer were bounding bye;   65
Upon the bow-string lies the shaft of death!
   Breathless impatience burns in every eye!
   At once a thousand winged arrows fly;
The grayhound up the glen outstrips the wind;
   At once the slow-hounds' music rends the sky,   70
The hunter's whoop and hallo cheers behind!
Haloo! away they speed! swift as the course of mind!

9.

There roll'd the bausin'd hind adown the linn,
   Transfix'd by arrow from the Border bow;
There the poor roe-deer quakes the cliff within,   75
   The silent gray-hound watching close below.
   But yonder far the chesnut rovers go,
O'er hill, o'er dale, they mock thy hounds and thee;
   Cheer, hunter, cheer! unbend thy cumbrous bow,
Bayard and blood-hound now thy hope must be,   80
Or soon they gain the steeps, and pathless woods of Dee.

10.

Halloo, o'er hill and dale! the slot is warm!
   To every cliff the bugle lends a bell;
On to the northward peals the loud alarm,
   And ay the brocket and the sorel fell: 85
   But flying still before the mingled yell,
The gallant herd outspeeds the troubled wind;
   Their rattling antlers brush the birken dell;
Their haughty eyes the rolling tear-drops blind;
But onward still they speed, and look not once behind!   90

11.

The Tilt is vanish'd on the upland gray,
   The Tarf is dwindled to a foaming rill;
But many a hound lay gasping by the way,
   Bathed in the stream, or stretch'd upon the hill;
   The cooling brook with burning jaws they swill,   95
Nor once will deign to scent the tainted ground:
   The herd has cross'd Breriach's gulfing gill,
The Athol forest's formidable bound,
And in the Garcharye a last retreat have found.

12.

One hound alone has cross'd the dreary height,   100
  The deep-toned Jowler, ever staunch and true.
The chace was o'er; but long ere fell the night,
    Full thirty hinds those gallant hunters slew,
    Of every age and kind; the drivers drew
Their quarry on behind by ford and lea: 105
  But never more shall eye of monarch view
So wild a scene of mountain majesty
As Scotland's King beheld from the tall peaks of Dee.

13.

On gray Macduich's upmost verge he stood,
  The loftiest cone of all that desart dun;   110
The seas afar were streamer'd o'er with blood!
    Dark forests waved, and winding waters run!
    For nature glow'd beneath the evening sun;
The western shadows dark'ning every dale,
  Where dens of gloom, the sight of man to shun,   115
Lay shrouded in impervious magic veil;
While o'er them pour'd the rays of light so lovely pale.

14.

But O what bard could sing the onward sight!
  The piles that frown'd, the gulfs that yawn'd beneath!
Downward a thousand fathoms from the height,   120
    Grim as the caverns in the land of death!
    Like mountains shatter'd in th' Eternal's wrath,
When fiends their banners 'gainst his reign unfurl'd—
  A grisly wilderness! a land of scathe!
Rocks upon rocks in dire confusion hurl'd!   125
A rent and formless mass, the rubbish of a world.

15.

As if by lost pre-eminence abased,
  Hill behind hill erected locks of gray,
And every misty morion was upraised,
    To speak their farewell to the God of Day: 130
    When tempests rave along their polar way,
Not closer rear the billows of the deep,
  Shining with silver foam, and maned with spray,
As up the mid-way heaven they war and sweep,
Then, foil'd and chafed to rage, roll down the broken steep.   135

16.

First died upon the peaks the golden hue,
    And o'er them spread a beauteous purple screen;
Then rose a shade of pale cerulean blue,
    Softening the hills and hazy vales between:
    Deeper and deeper grew the magic scene,   140
As darker shades of the night-heaven came on;
    No star along the firmament was seen,
But solemn majesty prevail'd alone
Around the brows of Eve, upon her Grampian throne.

17.

Steep the descent and rugged was the way   145
    By which the Monarch and his Knights came down,
And oft they groped and stumbled on the brae,
    For far below, on vale of heather brown,
    The tents were rear'd, and fires of evening shone:
The mountain sounds had perish'd in the gloom,   150
    All save th' unwearied Jowler's swelling tone,
That bore to trembling stag the sounds of doom,
While every cave of Night roll'd back the breathing boom.

18.

Th' impassion'd huntsman wended up the brae,
    And loud the order of desistance bawl'd;   155
But aye, as louder wax'd his tyrant's say,
    Louder and fiercer, Jowler, unappall'd,
    Across the glen, along the mountain brawl'd,
Unpractised he to part till blood was seen—
    Though sore by precipice and darkness gall'd,   160
He turn'd his dewlap to the starry sheen,
And howl'd in furious tone, with yelp and bay between.

19.

Well known that spot, once graced by sovereign's sleep,
    Still bears it the memorial of his name;
The silver torrent play'd his vesper deep,   165
    The mountain plover sung his loud acclaim!
    Inured to toil and battle's deadly flame,
The Stuart rose the son of health and might.
    Ah! how unlike the bland voluptuous frame
In this unthrifty age, that takes delight   170
To doze in qualms by day, and revel out the night!

20.

The Night had journey'd up the dark blue steep,
   And lean'd upon the casement of the sky,
Smiling serenely o'er a world in sleep,
    At millions of her wand'ring elfins sly;   175
    Harassing helpless mortals as they lie
With dreams and fantasies of endless train;
    With tantalizing sweets that mock the eye,
With startling horror, and with visions vain,
And every thrilling trance of pleasure and of pain.   180

21.

In mantle wrapt, and stretch'd on flowery heath,
   She saw the King of Scotland weary lie;
So deep his slumber, that the hand of death
    Arrests not more the reasoning faculty;
    Yet was his fancy rapt in passion high,   185
He toil'd with visions of a wayward dream;
    Quiver'd his limbs, his bosom broke the sigh,
He clasp'd the yielding heath, and named a name—
He would not for his crown to nobles' ear it came!

22.

The heavenly guardian of the royal head,   190
   That rules events and elements at will,
Unused in wilderness to watch his bed,
    Or spread his shelt'ring pinion on the hill,
    Unrife in circumstance foreboding ill,
Yet trembled for some danger lingering near.   195
    What gath'ring sound comes nigher, nigher still?
Why does the wakening hound turn up his ear,
Then start with shorten'd bark, and bristle all with fear?

23.

Fast gains th' alarm—the nobles, half awake,
   Restrain their breathing, mindless where they lie;   200
The sleepy ranger starts from out the brake,
    With mouth wide open and unvision'd eye;
    Knight, squire, and hind, in one direction fly,
Mix'd with the hounds that loud in couples bay,
    All to the downward burn that sounded bye,   205
For there arose the dubious, frantic bray,
That raised the dreamer's eye, and all that loud affray.

24.

O smile not at the confluent midnight scene,
   The blazing torch, the looks of wild dismay!—
It was no angry spirit of the glen,   210
   No murd'rous clansmen mix'd in red array:
   There stood the monarch of the wild at bay,
The impetuous Jowler howling at his brow,
   His cheeks all drench'd with brine, his antlers gray
Moving across the cliff, majestic slow,   215
Like living fairy trees of blench'd and leafless bough.

25.

With ruthless shaft they pierced his heaving breast,
   The baited, thirsty Jowler laps his blood;
The royal Hunter his brave hound caress'd,
   Lauded his zeal and spirit unsubdued;   220
   While the staunch victor, of approval proud,
Roll'd his brown back upon the prostrate slain,
   Caper'd around in playful whelpish mood,
As if unspent by all his toil and pain,
Then lick'd his crimson flew, and look'd to th' hills again. 225

26.

For three long days the deer were driven afar,
   And many a herd was thinn'd and sore bespent;
Through dark Glen-Avin, and the woods of Mar,
   Hart, hind, and roe in trembling trails were blent.
   Still in the wild remain'd the royal tent;   230
One little bothy stood behind the lea,
   Where oft at eve the King and nobles went
The setting sun and soaring erne to see,
Behind the dreadful cliffs that watch the springs of Dee.

27.

One eve they sat all in a jocund row,   235
   The cruel Knight of Souden he was one;
They noted horror staring on his brow,
   His lip was quivering, and his colour gone!
   And aye he look'd the startled knights upon,
Then roll'd his troubled glance along the hill.   240
   "What moves thee?" said the King, in mildest tone.
He bow'd his head, but held his silence still.
"What moves my gallant knight? Speak, Souden, art thou ill?"

28.

"My sovereign liege, forgiveness I implore;
  Strange recollections dim my palsied sight;   245
But this same dreary scene I've seen before,
  Either in trance, or vision of the night.
  Some dismal doom shall soon my honours blight;
I know these bodings fraught with woe to be.
  It seems as demon dragg'd a deed to light,   250
That lies unfathom'd even to destiny!"–
O ne'er may leil man keep with murderer company!

29.

No more he spoke that eve, as legends tell;
  No orders issued to his page or groom;
But servitors, with trembling, mark'd full well   255
  A wondrous face behind him in the gloom;
  Of flame it seem'd, yet nothing did illume;
Laughing, revenge gleam'd red in every line:
  But how it enter'd the pavilion'd room,
Or how it past, no mortal could divine!   260
A visitant it seem'd from some unhallow'd shrine!

30.

Again the low'ring clouds immure the hill;
  Again the sportsmen stretch their limbs in rest;
To the lone bothy, by the sounding rill,
  The King retired, its wildness pleased him best,   265
  With his good knights to list the song and jest;
His ancient minstrel waiting at command,
  Gilbert of Sheil, by all the land confest
A minstrel worthy by his King to stand,
And play his native airs, with sounding harp in hand.   270

31.

That evening, call'd to sing, he framed a lay,–
  A lay of such mysterious tendency,
It stole the listeners' reasoning powers away;
  They dream'd not that they lay in moors of Dee,
  But in some fairy isle amid the sea,   275
So well did Fancy mould her visions vain:
  Bent was the minstrel's eye, and wild to see,
As thus he pour'd the visionary strain.
O ne'er shall Grampian echo murmur such again!

The Harper's Song

There wals ane auld caryl wonit in yon howe, 280
  Lemedon! lemedon! ayden lillelu!
His face was the geire, and his hayre was the woo,
  Sing Ho! Ro! Gillan of Allanhu!
But och! quhan the mure getis his cuerlet gray, &c.
Quhan the gloamyng hes flauchtit the nychte and the
    day, &c. 285
Quhan the crawis haif flowin to the greinwode schaw,
And the kydde hes blet owr the Lammer Law;
Quhan the dewe hes layde the klaiver asteep,
And the gowin hes fauldit hir buddis to sleep;
Quhan nochte is herde but the merlinis mene— 290
Och! than that gyre caryl is neuir his lene!

  Ane bonnye baby, se meike and mylde,
Ay walkis wythe hym the dowie wylde:
The gowlin getis of sturt and stryffe,
And wearie wailis of mortyl lyffe, 295
Wald all be hushit till endlesse pece
At ane blynke of that babyis fece!

  Hir browe se fayre, and her ee se meike,
And the damyske roz that blumis on her cheike;
Hir lockis, and the bend of her bonnye bree, 300
And hir smyle mochte waukin the deide to see!

  Hir snoode, befryngit with mony a geme,
Wals stouin fra the raynbowe's brychtest beme;
And hir raile, mair quhyte than snawye dryfte,
Wals neuir wovin anethe the lyfte; 305
It keust sikn lychte on hill and gaire,
It shawit the wylde deer til hir laire;
And the fayries wakinit fra their beddis of dewe,
And they sang ane hyme, and the hyme was new!
List, lordyngs, list! for neuir agayne 310
Shalt' heire sikn wylde wanyirdlye strayne.
For they sang the nychte-gale in ane swoone,
And they sang the goud lockes fra the moone;
They sang the reidbreiste fra the wud,
And the laueroke out of the merlit clud; 315
And sum wee feres of bludeless byrthe

Cam out of the wurmholes of the yirthe,
And swoofit se lychtlye round the lee,
That they waldna kythe to mortyl ee;
But their erlisch sang it rase se shill,   320
That the waesum tod youlit on the hill!
O lordyngs, list the cronach blande!
The flycherynge songe of Fayrie-land!

The Song of the Fairies

SING AYDEN! AYDEN! LILLELU!
Bonnye bairne, we sing to you!   325
Up the Quhyte, and doune the Blak,
No ane leuer, no ane lak,
No ane shado at ouir bak;
No ane stokyng, no ane schue,
No ane bendit blever blue,   330
No ane traissel in the dewe!
Bonnye bairn, we sing to you,
AYDEN! AYDEN! LILLELU! &c.

    Speile! speile!
     The moone-rak speile!   335
Warre the rowar, warre the steile,
Throu the rok and throu the reile,
Rounde about lyke ane spynning wheile;
Throu the libbert, throu the le,
Rounde the yirde and rounde the se,   340
Bonnye bairne, we sing to thee,
Rounde the blumis and bellis of dewe,
AYDEN! AYDEN! LILLELU!

    Speide! speide!
     Lyving or deide!   345
Faster than the fyirie gleide,
Biz throu Laplin's tyrling dryfte!
Rounde the moone, and rounde the lyfte,
Aye we ring, and aye we sing
Our hune! hune!   350
And ante-tune!
Neuir! neuir! neuir dune!
Up the Leider and doune the Dye
Ay we sing our lullabye!

Bonnye bairne, we sing to you, 355
AYDEN! AYDEN! LILLELU!

    Ryng! ryng!
  Daunce and sing!
Hiche on the brume yer garlandis hyng!
For the bairnis sleipe is sweite and sure, 360
And the maydenis reste is blist and pure
Throu all the lynkis of Lammer-mure;
Sen our bonnye baby was sent fra heven.
Scho comis owrnycht withe the dewe of even,
And quhan the sone keikes out of the maine, 365
Scho swawis with the dewe to heven again.
But the lychte shall dawne and the houlat flee,
The deide shall ake, and the day shall be
Quhan scho shall smyle in the gladsum noone,
And sleipe and sleipe in the lychte of the moone! 370
Then shall our luias weke anewe,
With herpe and vele and ayril too,
To AYDEN! AYDEN! LILLELU!

    Hyde! hyde!
  Quhateuir betyde, 375
Elfe and dowle that ergh to byde!
The littil wee burdie mai cheipe in the wa,
The plevir mai sing, and the coke mai craw;
For neuir ane spyrit derke and doure
Dar raike the creukis of Lammer-mure; 380
And everilke gaiste of gysand hue
Shall melt in the breize our baby drew!
But we ar left in the grein-wud glen,
Bekaus we luf the chylder of men,
Sweitlye to sing our flawmand new; 385
Bonnye bairne, we sing to you,
AYDEN! AYDEN! LILLELU!

    Pace! pace!
  Spyritis of grace!
Sweite is the smyle of our babyis face! 390
The kelpye dernis, in dreide and dule,
Deipe in the howe of his eirye pule;
Gil-Moules frehynde the hallen mene fle,
Throu the dor-threshil, and throu the dor-ke,
And the mer-mayde mootes in the saifrone se. 395

But we ar left in the greine-wud glen,
Bekaus we luf the chylder of men,
Sweitlye to sing and neuir to rue,
Sweitlye to sing our last adue;
Bonnye bairne, we sing to you,   400
AYDEN! AYDEN! LILLELU!

    Sing! sing!
   How shall we sing
Rounde the bairne of the spiritis Kyng!
Lillelu! lillelu! mount in a ryng!   405
Fayries away! away on the wyng!
We too maune flytt to ane land of blisse!
To ane land of holy silentnesse!
To ane land quhair the nycht-wynd neuir blewe!
But thy fayre spryng shall euir be newe!   410
Quhan the moone shall waik ne mayre to wane,
And the clud and the raynbowe baithe are gane,
In bowirs aboone the brik of the day
We'll sing to our baby for ever and ay!

Than the caryl he saw them swoof alang,   415
And he herde the wordis of thair leifu sang;
They seemit to lyng asklent the wynde,
And left ane streamourie trak behynde;
But he heirit them singyng as they flew,
AYDEN! AYDEN! LILLELU!   420

Than the caryl liftit the babe se yung,
And nemit hir with ane tremilous tung;
And the lychte of God strak on his face
As he nelit on the dewe, and callit her Grace:
And he barrit the day of sorrowe and reuth   425
To flee fra the bairne of Hevenly Truthe;
And he barrit the deidis that nurice paine
Euir to thrall the worild again.
Than he claspit his handis, and wepit ful sair,
Quhan he bade hir adue for evirmaire.   430
O neuir wals babyis smyle se meike
Quhan scho fand the teir drap on her cheike!
And neuir wals babyis leuke se wae

Quhan scho saw the leil auld caryl gae!
But all his eiless ouphen trayne,   435
And all his gaistis and gyis war gane;
The gleides that gleimit in the derksome schaw,
And his fayries had flown the last of a':
Than the puir auld caryl was blythe to fle
Away fra the emerant isle of the se,   440
And neuir mayre seikis the walkis of men,
Unless in the diske of the glomyng glen.

32.

The harper ceased; the chords, with sighing tone,
   On list'ners' ears in soft vibrations fell;
They almost ween'd they heard the parting moan   445
   Of the old reverend sire, and wish'd him well!—
   On gospel faith, and superstition's spell,
The converse turn'd, and high the dispute ran;
   And words were said unfitting bard to tell;
Unfitting tongue of poor despondent man,   450
Still prone to yearn and doubt o'er all he cannot scan.

33.

To what unsaintly goal the words had borne,
   Dubious conjecture only can pourtray:
Just in the blab of Souden's impious scorn
   Enter'd a stranger guest in poor array!   455
   His locks were thin, and bleach'd a silver gray;
His reverend beard across his girdle hung.
   Each mind was carried, by resistless sway,
To the old carl of whom the minstrel sung.
Blench'd was the proudest cheek, and mute was every
    tongue!   460

34.

He stood erect, but raised not up his eye,
   Seeming to listen for expected sound;
But all was still as Night's solemnity,
   Not even a sandal grazed upon the ground.
   Transform'd to breathing statues, all around   465
The nobles sat, nor wist they what to dread;
   But every sense by hand unseen was bound,
On every valiant heart was chillness shed,
As to that wild had come a message from the dead.

35.

At length to Scotland's Monarch rose his look,   470
   On whom he beckon'd with commanding mien,
With manner that denial would not brook,
   Then gliding forth he paused upon the green.
   What the mysterious messenger could mean
No one would risk conjecture; all were still.   475
   In converse close, the two were lingering seen
Across the lea, and down beside the rill,
Then seem'd to vanish both in shadow of the hill.

36.

And never more was seen the royal face
   By Athol forest or the links of Dee!   480
O why should haughty worm of human race
   Presume to question Heaven's supremacy!
   Or trow his God, alike unmoved, can see
To death exposed the monarch and the clown!
   That night was done, by the supreme decree,   485
A deed that story scarce may dare to own!
By what unearthly hand, to all mankind unknown!

37.

At midnight, strange disturbing sounds awoke
   The drowsy slumberers on the tented heath.
It was no blast, that on the mountain broke!   490
   Nor bolised thunder wrapt in sable wrath!
   Yet were they listening, with suspended breath,
To hear the rushing tumult once again:
   It seem'd to all the passing sounds of death,
Or angry spirits of the mountain reign,   495
Combined at midnight deep to clear their wild domain.

38.

Six gallant yeomen rose, and, hand to hand,
   Set forth the bothy's wild recess to gain;
Despising fate, and monarch's strict command,
   That all should quiet at the tents remain: 500
   They harbour'd fears that tongue could not explain.
Darkling and silent, midway on they past,
   When power unseen their passage did restrain;
Each onward step they deem'd would be their last,
And backward traced their path, unboastful and aghast.   505

39.

The morning came, in pall of sackcloth veil'd;
  The cliffs of Dee a sable vestment bound;
Then every squire and yeoman's spirit fail'd,
  As slow approach'd a maim'd and bleeding hound.
Sad herald of the dead! his every wound   510
Bespoke the desolation that was wrought!—
  O ne'er may scene in Scottish glen be found
With wonder, woe, and death so fully fraught!
So far beyond the pale of bounded mortal thought!

40.

No knight walk'd forth to taste the morning air,   515
  The bugle's echo slept within the hill!
And—O the blasting truth!—no cot was there!
  No! not a vestige stood beside the rill!
  Though trace of element, or human skill,
In all the fatal glen could not be found,   520
  The ghastly forms, in prostrate guise and still,
Knight, page, and hound, lay scatter'd far around,
Deform'd by many a stain, and deep unseemly wound.

41.

The King was sought by many an anxious eye;—
  No King was there!—Well might the wonder grow! 525
They rode—they search'd the land afar and nigh—
  He was not found, nor learn'd the tale of woe!—
  Hast thou not mark'd a lonely spot and low,
Where Moulin opes her bosom to the day,
  O'er which the willow weeps and birches blow, 530
Where nine rude stones erect their frontlets gray?—
There the blasphemers lie, slain in mysterious way.

42.

When nine long days were past, and all was o'er;
  When round his nobles slain had closed the mould,
The King return'd to Scotland's court once more, 535
  And wonder'd at the tale his huntsmen told:
  His speech revolted, and his blood ran cold,
As low he kneel'd at good Saint Bothan's shrine.
  Where he had been no tongue did e'er unfold.—
List to my tale!—if thou can'st nought divine, 540
A slow misfashion'd mind, a moody soul is thine.

Mador of the Moor

Canto Second

The Minstrel

Argument

There cam a fiddler here to play,
And O but he was gimp an' gay;
He staw the lassie's heart away,
An' made it a' his ain O.

For weel he kend the way O, the way O, the way O,
Weel he kend the way O, the lassie's love to gain O.

Mador of the Moor

Canto Second

The Minstrel

1.

THAT time there lived upon the banks of Tay
    A man of right ungainly courtesy;
Yet he was aident in his froward way,
    And honest as a Highlander may be.
    He was not man of rank, nor mean degree,   5
And loved his spouse, and child, as such became;
    Yet oft would fret, and wrangle irefully,
Fastening on them of every ill the blame,
Nor list the loud defence of his unyielding dame.

2.

She was unweeting, plump, and fair to see;   10
    Dreadless of ills she ne'er before had seen;
Full of blithe jolliment and boisterous glee:
    Yet was her home not well bedight or clean;
    For, like the most of all her sex, I ween,
Much she devised, but little did conclude;   15
    Much toil was lost, as if it ne'er had been.
Her tongue was fraught with matter wonderous crude,
And, in her own defence, most voluble and loud.

3.

But O the lovely May,* their only child,
    Was sweeter than the flower that scents the gale!   20
Her lightsome form, and look so soothing mild,
    The loftiest minstrel song would much avale;
    And she was cheerful, forwardsome and hale;
And she could work the rich embroidery,
    Or with her maidens bear the milking pail;   25
Yet, dight at beltane reel, you could espy
No lady in the land who with this May could vie.

---

* A May, in old Scottish ballads and romances, denotes a young
  lady, or a maiden somewhat above the lower class.

4.

And many a younker sigh'd her love to gain;
   Her steps were haunted at the bught and penn;
But all their prayers and vows of love were vain,   30
   Her choice was fix'd on Albert of the Glen:
   No youth was he, nor winsomest of men,
For he was proud, and full of envy's gall;
   But what was lovelier to the damsel's ken,
He had wide lands, and servants at his call;   35
Her sire was liegeman bound, and held of him his all.

5.

The beauteous May, to parents' will resign'd,
   Opposed not that which boded nothing ill;
It gave an ease and freedom to her mind,
   And wish, the anxious interval to kill: 40
   She listed wooer's tale with right goodwill;
And she would jest, and smile, and heave the sigh;
   Would torture whining youth with wicked skill,
Turn on her heel, then off like lightning fly,
Leaving the hapless wight resolved forthwith to die.   45

6.

The rainbow's lovely in the eastern cloud;
   The rose is beauteous on the bended thorn;
Sweet is the evening ray from purple shroud,
   And sweet the orient blushes of the morn;
   Sweeter than all, the beauties which adorn   50
The female form in youth and maiden bloom!
   O why should passion ever man suborn
To work the sweetest flower of Nature's doom,
And cast o'er all her joys a veil of cheerless gloom!

7.

O fragile flower! that blossoms but to fade!   55
   One slip recovery or recal defies!
Thou walk'st the dizzy verge with steps unstaid,
   Fair as the habitants of yonder skies!
   Like them, thou fallest never more to rise!
O fragile flower! for thee my heart's in pain!   60
   Haply a world is hid from mortal eyes,
Where thou may'st smile in purity again,
And shine in virgin bloom, that ever shall remain.

8.

The twentieth spring had breathed upon the flower,
    Nor had that flower pass'd with the year away,   65
Since first the infant bloom of Ila Moore,
    The flower of Athol, open'd to the day.
    Kincraigy was her home, that o'er the Tay
A prospect held of Nature's fairest scene,–
    Far mountains mixing with aërial gray,   70
Low golden-vested vallies stretch'd between,
And far below the eye, broad flood and islet green.

9.

The day was wet, the mist was on the moor,
    Rested from labour husbandman and maid;
There came a Stranger to Kincraigy's door   75
    Of goodly form, in minstrel garb array'd;
    Of braided silk his builziment was made:
Short the entreatance he required to stay!
    He tuned his viol, and with veh'mence play'd;
Mistress and menial, maid and matron gray,   80
Soon mix'd were on the floor, and frisk'd in wild affray.

10.

The Minstrel strain'd and twisted sore his face,
    Beat with his heel, and twinkled with his eye,
But still, at every effort and grimace,
    Louder and quicker rush'd the melody: 85
    The dancers round the floor in mazes fly,
With cheering whoop, and wheel, and caper wild
    The jolly dame did well her mettle ply!
Even old Kincraigy, of his spleen beguiled,
Turn'd his dark brow aside, soften'd his looks and smiled. 90

11.

When supper on the ashen board was set,
    The Minstrel, all unask'd, jocosely came,
Brought his old chair, and, without pause or let,
    Placed it betwixt the maid and forthright dame.
    They smiled, and asked his lineage and his name–   95
'Twas Mador of the Moor, a name renown'd!
    A kindred name with theirs, well known to fame,–
A high-born name! but old Kincraigy frown'd,
Such impudence in man, he ween'd, had not been found.

12.

The last red embers on the hearth were spread,   100
    But Mador still his antick tricks pursued;
The doors were closed, and all were bound to bed,
    When, spite of old Kincraigy's angry mood,
    The frantic hurlyburly was renew'd:
His tongue grew mute, his face o'erspread with gloom;   105
    Wild uproar raged resistless, unsubdued;
The younkers of the hamlet crowd the room,
And Mador's viol squeaks, with rough and raging boom!

13.

The dire misrule Kincraigy could not brook;
    He saw distinction lost, and order spurn'd;   110
And, much displeased that his offended look
    Was all uminded, high his anger burn'd.
    Upon the rocket Minstrel dark he turn'd,
And ask'd to whom such strains he wont to play?—
    O! he had play'd to nobles now inurn'd!   115
And he had play'd in countries far away,
And to the gallant King that o'er them held the sway!

14.

"Ay!" said Kincraigy, with malignant scowl,
    Stroking his beard and writhing down his brow;
"I've heard our Monarch was an arrant fool!   120
    I ween'd it so, but knew it not till now!
    But 'tis enough!—his choice of such as you!—
Great heaven! to man what inconsistence clings!
    To meanest of the species doom'd to bow!
Had I one day o'er all created things,   125
The world should once be clear'd of fiddlers and of kings!"

15.

'Twas a hard jest; but Mador laugh'd it bye;
    Across the strings his careless fingers stray'd,
Till staunch Kincraigy, with unalter'd eye,
    Ask'd how, or where, he learn'd the scraping trade?   130
    When those new jars to music came allayed?
And how it happ'd he in the line had thriven?
    For sure, of all the fiddlers ever play'd,
Never was bow by such a novice driven,
Never were human ears by such discordance riven.   135

16.

Go tell the monarch of his feelings cold;
　　Go tell the prince that he is lewd and vain;
Go tell the wrinkled maid that she is old,
　　The wretched miser of his ill-got gain;
　　But O! in human kindness, spare the pain　　　　140
That conscious excellence abased must feel!
　　It proves to wounded pride the deadliest bane!
The judgment it arraigns, and stamps the seal
Of *fool* with burning brand, which blood alone can heal.

17.

The earliest winter hues of old Cairn-Gorm,　　　　145
　　Schehallion when the clouds begin to lour,
Even the wan face of heaven before the storm,
　　Look'd ne'er so stern as Mador of the Moor.
　　Most cutting sharp was his retort and sour,
And in offensive guise his bow he drew.　　　　　　150
　　Kincraigy redden'd, stepp'd across the floor,
Lifted his staff, and back indignant flew
To scathe the Minstrel's pate, and baste him black and blue.

18.

Had those to Mador known in royal hall,
　　(For well I ween he was not stranger there,)　　155
Beheld him crouching 'gainst that smoky wall,
　　His precious violin heaved high in air,
　　As guardian shield, the ireful blow to bear;
The blowzy dame holding with all her might
　　An interceding maid so lovely fair;　　　　　　160
Matron and peasant gaping with affright—
O 'twas a scene of life might charm an anchorite!

19.

'Twas not the fluster'd dame's inept rebuke,
　　'Twas not the cowering Minstrel's perilous state,
'Twas beauteous Ila Moore's reproving look　　　　165
　　That quell'd her sire, and barr'd the work of fate:
　　With smile serene she led him to his seat,
Sat by his knee, and bade the Minstrel play.
　　No word was heard of anger or debate,
So much may woman's eye our passions sway!　　　170
When beauty gives command, all mankind must obey!

20.

The wearied peasants to their rest retire;
  Kincraigy bows to sleep's resistless call;
But the kind dame stirr'd up the sluggish fire,
  And with the Minstrel long outsat them all;   175
  He praised her much, her order, and her hall,—
Her manners, far above her rank and place!
  Her daughter's beauteous form, so comely tall!
The peerless charms of her bewitching face,
So well befitting court, or noble's hall to grace.   180

21.

Well may'st thou trust the chicken with the dam;
  The eaglet in her parents' home sublime;
The yeaning ewe with the poor starveling lamb;
  Nor is a son's default a mother's crime:
  But a fair only daughter in her prime,   185
O never trust to mother's wistful care!
  The heart's too anxious of her darling's time:
Too well she loves—too well she is aware
In what the maid delights, nor sees the lurking snare.

22.

Aloft was framed the Minstrel's humble bed   190
  Of the green braken and the yielding heath,
With coverlet of dowlas o'er it spread;—
  That too he lauded with obsequious breath.
  But he was out, and in—above—beneath,
Unhinging doors, and groping in the dark: 195
  The hamlet matrons dread unearthly scathe;
The maidens hide their heads, the watch-dogs bark,
And all was noise and fright till matin of the lark.

23.

Next day the wind from eastern oceans drove
  The drizzly sea-rack up the Athol plain,   200
And o'er the woodland and the welkin wove
  A moving mantle of the fleecy rain:
  The cottagers from labour still refrain;
Well by the lowly window could they spy
  The droplets from the thatch descend amain;   205
While round the hearth they closed with cheerful eye,
Resolved, on better days, with all their might to ply.

24.

Though many hints, to make the Minstrel budge,
　　Were by Kincraigy thrown, they were in vain:
He ask'd him where that night he meant to lodge?　　210
　　And when he purposed calling there again?—
　　He could not stir!—the hateful driving rain
Would all his valued tuneful chords undo.
　　The dame reproach'd her husband's surly strain,
Welcomed the Minstrel's stay, and 'gan to show　　215
Her excellence in song, and skill in music too.

25.

Woe to the hapless wight, self-doom'd to see
　　His measures warp'd by woman's weak controul!
Woe to the man, whate'er his wealth may be,
　　Condemn'd to prove the everlasting growl,　　220
　　The fret, the plaint, the babble, and the scowl!
Yet such outnumber all the stars above!
　　When sponsal'd pairs run counter, soul to soul,
O there's an end to all the sweets of love!
That ray of heavenly bliss, which reason should improve. 225

26.

The dance and song prevail'd till fell the night;
　　The Minstrel's forward ease advanced apace;
He kiss'd their lovely May before their sight,
　　Who struggled, smiling, from the rude embrace,
　　And call'd him fiddler Mador to his face.　　230
Loud laugh'd the dame, while old Kincraigy frown'd.
　　Her fulsome levity, and flippant grace,
Had oft inflicted on his soul the wound,
But held at endless bay, redress could not be found.

27.

All quietness and peace our Minstrel spurns;　　235
　　Idle confusion through the hamlet rings;
He teazes, flatters, and cajoles by turns,
　　And to the winds all due distinction flings.
　　From his rude grasp the cottage matron springs,
The giggling maids in darksome corners hide;　　240
　　But still to Ila Moore he fondly clings,
Seeming resolved, whatever might betide,
To teaze or flatter her, and all reserve deride.

28.

Next day, by noon, the mountain's misty shroud
    The bustling spirits of the air updrew,   245
And 'gan to open in the boreal cloud
    Their marbled windows of the silvery hue;
    Far through the bores appear'd the distant blue;
Loud sung the merl upon the topmost spray;
    The harping bleeter, and the gray curlew,   250
High in the air chanted incondite lay;
All heralding th' approachment of a beauteous day.

29.

The Minstrel to the forest turn'd his eye,
    He seem'd regretful that the rain should stay;
He seem'd to wish the mist would lingering lye   255
    Still on the bosom of the moorland gray.
    The time was come he needs must wend his way,
His Sovereign's pleasure might his presence claim.
    No one remain'd to row him o'er the Tay,
Unless the blooming May or cordial dame.   260
The Tay was broad and deep—pray was the maid to blame?

30.

Westward they past by bank and greenwood side,
    A varied scene it was of wonderous guise;
Below them parting rivers smoothly glide,
    And far above their heads aspiring rise   265
    Gray crested rocks, the columns of the skies,
While little lowly dells lay hid between:
    It seem'd a fairy land! a paradise!
Where every bloom that scents the woodland green
Open'd to Heaven its breast by human eye unseen.   270

31.

Queen of the forest, there the birch tree swung
    Her light green locks aslant the southern breeze;
Red berries of the brake around them hung;
    A thousand songsters warbled on the trees:
    A scene it was befitting youth to please.   275
Too well it pleased, as reverend legends say!
    Unmark'd the hour o'er lovers' head that flees!
'Twas but one little mile!—a summer day!
And when the sun went down they scarce had reach'd the Tay!

32.

O read not, lovers!–sure you may not think   280
  That Ila Moore by minstrel airs was won!
'Twas nature's cordial glow, the kindred link
  That all unweeting chains two hearts in one!–
  Then why should mankind ween the maid undone,
Though with her youth she seek the woodland deep,   285
  Rest in a bower to view the parting sun,
Lean on his breast, at tale of woe to weep,
Or sweetly, on his arm, recline in mimic sleep?

33.

O I have seen, and fondly blest the sight,
  The peerless charms of maiden's guileful freak!   290
Through the dark eye-lash peep the orb so bright;
  The wily features so demurely meek;
  The smile of love half dimpling on the cheek;
The quaking breast, that heaves the sigh withal!
  The parting lips which more than language speak!–   295
Of fond delights, which memory can recall,
O beauty's feigned sleep far, far outdoes them all!

34.

O'er such a sleep the enamour'd Minstrel hung,
  Stole one soft kiss, but still she sounder fell!
The half-form'd sentence died upon her tongue;   300
  'Twas through her sleep she spoke!–Pray was it well,
  Molesting helpless maiden in the dell,
On sweet restoring slumber so intent?
  Our Minstrel framed resolve I joy to tell;
'Twas, not to harm that beauteous innocent,   305
For no delight, nor joy, that fancy might present.

35.

When at the ferry, silent long they stood,
  And eyed the red-beam on the pool that lay,
Or baseless shadow of the waving wood.–
  That lonely spot, upon the banks of Tay,   310
  Still bears the maiden's name, and shall for aye.
Warm was the parting sigh their bosoms drew!
  For sure, the joys of that enchanting day,
'Twas worth an age of sorrow to renew!
Then, glancing oft behind, they sped along the dew.   315

36.

Oft did Kincraigy's wayward humour keep
　The hamlet and the hall in teazing broil;
But his reproaches never cut so deep
　As when, that eve, he ceased his rural toil:
　He learn'd the truth, and raised such grievous coil　　320
That even the dame in rage gave up defence:
　The lovely cause of all the wild turmoil
Sat in a corner, grieved for her offence,
Offering no urgent plea, nor any false pretence.

37.

When summer suns around the zenith glow,　　325
　Nature is gaudy, frolicsome, and boon;
But when September breezes cease to blow,
　And twilight steals beneath the broaden'd moon,
　How changed the scene!—the year's resplendent noon
Is long gone past, and all is mildly still;　　330
　Sedateness settles on the dale and doone;
Wan is the flow'ret by the mountain rill,
And a pale boding look sits solemn on the hill.

38.

More changed than all the mien of Ila Moore!
　Scarce could you trow the self-same soul within:　　335
The buxom lass that loved the revel hour,
　That laugh'd at all, and grieved for nought but sin,
　Steals from her darling frolic, jest, and din,
And sits alone beneath the fading tree;
　Upon her bosom leans her dimpled chin;　　340
Her moisten'd eye fix'd moveless on the lea,
Or vagrant tiny moth that sojourn'd on her knee.

39.

Her songs, that erst did scarcely maid become,
　So framed they were of blandishment and jest,
Were changed into a soft unmeaning hum,　　345
　A sickly melody, yet unexpress'd.
　At tale of pity throbb'd her ardent breast;
The tear was ready for mishap or joy!
　And well she loved in evening grove to rest,
To tender Heaven her vow without annoy,　　350
Indulging secret thought—a thought that did not cloy.

40.

The dame perceived the maiden's alter'd mood;
  A dame of keen distinguishment was she!
And O her measures were most wond'rous shrewd!
  And deeply schemed, as woman's needs must be,   355
  Though all the world with little toil could see
Her latent purposes from first to last.
  An ancient Friar, who shrived the family,
She call'd into her chamber—barr'd it fast,
That listener might not hear th' important words that past.

41.

"Father, you mark'd the gallant Minstrel youth
  Who lately to the forest past this way;
I ween, he proffer made of hand and troth
  To our own child, and hardly would take nay.
  Put on thy humble cowl and frock of gray;   365
Thy order and array thy warrant be;
  And watch the royal tent at close of day,
It stands in glen, below the wells of Dee,
Note all entreatment there, and bring the truth to me.

42.

"Young Mador of the Moor, thou know'st him well;   370
  Mark thou what rank he holds, and mark aright:
If with the squires or vulgar grooms he dwell,
  If in the outer tent he sleeps by night,
  Regard him not, nor wait the morning light;
But if with royalty or knighthood set,   375
  Beckon him forth, in seeming serious plight,
And say, what most will his impatience whet,
That for his sake some cheeks are ever, ever wet!"

43.

Next morn, while yet the eastern mountains threw
  Their giant shadows o'er the slumbering dale,   380
Their darken'd verges trembling on the dew
  In rosy wreath, so lovely and so pale,
  The warp'd and slender rainbow of the vale!
Ere beauteous Ila's foot had prest the floor,
  Or her fair cheek had kiss'd the morning gale,   385
A lively rap came to Kincraigy's door—
There stood the active Friar, and Mador of the Moor!

44.

Well knew the dame this speed betoken'd good!
  But when she learn'd that Mador consort held
With majesty and knights of noblest blood,   390
  One of the select number in the field,
  Her courtesy no blandishment withheld.
Fair Ila trembled like the aspin bough,
  She dreaded passions guidelessly impell'd—
'Twas what of all the world she wish'd; yet now   395
A weight her heart oppress'd, she felt she wist not how!

45.

Kincraigy growl'd like hunted wolf at bay,
  And in his fields from outrage sought relief;
No burning fiend, whom convent wights gainsay,
  No ruthless abbey reave, nor Ranoch thief,   400
  Did ever work him such chagrin and grief
As did the Minstrel's smooth obtrusive face.
  Albert of Glen, his kind but haughty chief,
He saw exposed to infamous disgrace,
Himself to loss of name, of honour, and of place!   405

46.

His rage avail'd not—each reflective hint
  Was treated by his knowing dame with scorn,
Whose every word, and every action, went
  To show him his discernment was forlorn.
  He knew no more of life than babe unborn!   410
'Twas well some could distinguish who was who!
  Kincraigy's years were cumber'd and outworn
In manful strife his mastery to show,
Though forced on every point his priv'lege to forego.

47.

The Minstrel's table was with viands spread,   415
  His cup was fill'd though all the rest were dry;
Not on the floor was made the Minstrel's bed,
  He got the best Kincraigy could supply;
  While every day the former did outvie
In idle frolic round Kincraigy's hall: 420
  His frugal meal is changed to luxury;
His oxen low unnoted in the stall;
Loud revelry pervades, and lords it over all.

48.

The blooming May, from his first fond embrace,
   Shrunk pale and sullen, as from insult high;   425
A nameless dread was settled on her face;
   She fear'd the Minstrel, yet she knew not why.
   That previous night, when closed was every eye,
O she had dream'd of grievous scenes to be!
   And she had heard a little plaintive cry!   430
And she had sung beneath the willow tree,
And seen a rueful sight, unfitting maid to see!

49.

But when he told her of his fix'd resolve,
   That, should they not in wedlock ties be bound,
He never would that loving breast involve   435
   In rankling crime, nor pierce it with a wound,—
   It was so generous! she no longer frown'd,
But sighing sunk upon his manly breast.
   Sweet tender sex! with snares encompass'd round!
On others hang thy comforts and thy rest!   440
Child of dependence born, and failings unconfest!

50.

At eve, they lean'd upon the flowery sward,
   On fairy mound that overlooks the Tay;
And in the greenwood bowers of sweet Kinnaird
   They sought a refuge from the noontide ray: 445
   In bowers that scarce received the light of day,
Far, far below a rock's stupendous pile,
   In raptures of the purest love they lay,
While tender tale would intervals beguile—
Woe to the venal Friar, won to religious wile!   450

51.

If pure and full terrestrial bliss may be,
   And human imperfection that enjoy,
Those twain, beneath the deep embowering tree,
   Bathed in that perfect bliss without alloy.
   But passion's flame will passion's self destroy,   455
Such imperfections round our nature lour;
   No bliss is ours, that others mayn't annoy.
So happ'd it to Kincraigy's beauteous flower,
And eke her gay gallant, young Mador of the Moor.

52.

Albert of Glen, o'er his betrothed bride,   460
    Kept jealous eye, and oft unnoted came;
He saw the Minstrel ever by her side,
    And how his presence flush'd the bustling dame.
    Enraged at such a fond ungrateful flame,
One eve he caught them lock'd in fond embrace;   465
    And, bent his amorous rival's pride to tame,
Began with sandal'd foot, and heavy mace,
To work the Minstrel woe, and very deep disgrace.

53.

Few and unpolish'd were the words that past;
    Hard was the struggle and infuriate grasp!   470
But Mador of the Moor, o'erborne at last,
    Beneath his rival's frame began to gasp;
    His slender nape was lock'd in keyless hasp:
A maid's exertion saved him as before:
    Her willing fingers made the hands unclasp   475
That soon had still'd the struggling Minstrel's core—
He ne'er had flatter'd dame, nor courted maiden more.

54.

The swords were drawn, but neither jeer nor threat
    Could drive the fearless maiden from between;
Again her firmness quell'd the dire debate,   480
    And drove the ruffian from their bower of green.
    But grim and resolute revenge was seen
In his dark eye as furious he withdrew;
    And Mador of the Moor, his life to screen,
Escaped by night, through shades of murky hue: 485
The maiden deem'd it meet, for Albert well she knew.

55.

And well it proved for him!—At woman's schemes
    And deep-laid policy the jeer is due;
But for resource, and courage in extremes,
    For prompt expedient, and affection true,   490
    Distrust her not—ev'n though her means are few,
She will defeat the utmost powers of man;
    In strait, she never yet distinction drew
'Twixt right and wrong, nor squeamishly began
To calculate, or weigh, save how to gain her plan.   495

56.

Albert of Glen, with twenty warriours came,
  Beset Kincraigy's hall, and search'd it through;
Like the chafed ocean storm'd the fluster'd dame,
  Of Mador's hasty flight she did not know.
  Kincraigy hoped they would the wight undo;   500
In his malicious grin was joyance seen.
  Albert is baulk'd of sweet revenge, and now
Blazes outright a chieftain's smother'd spleen;
And Mador's lost and gone, as if he ne'er had been.

Mador of the Moor
Canto Third

The Cottage

Argument

O waly, waly, but love be bonny,
  A little while when it is new!
But when 'tis old it waxes cold,
  An' fades away like morning dew.
But had I wist before I kiss'd,
  That love had been sae ill to win,
I had lock'd my heart in a case o' goud,
  An' pinn'd it wi' a siller pin.

Mador of the Moor
Canto Third

The Cottage

1.

WHAT art thou, Love? or who may thee define?
  Where lies thy bourn of pleasure or of pain?
No sceptre, graved by Reason's hand, is thine,
    Child of the moisten'd eye and burning brain,
    Of glowing fancy, and the fervid vein,   5
That soft on bed of roses loves to rest,
    And crop the flower where lurks the deadly bane!
O many a thorn those dear delights invest,
Child of the rosy cheek, and heaving snow-white breast!

2.

Thou art the genial balm of virtuous youth,   10
    And point'st where Honour waves her wreath on high;
Like the sweet breeze that wanders from the south,
    Thou breath'st upon the soul, where embryos lie
    Of new delights, the treasures of the sky!
Who knows thy trembling watch in bower of even,   15
    Thy earliest grateful tear, and melting sigh?
O never was to yearning mortal given
So dear delights as thine, thou habitant of heaven!

3.

Woe that thy regal sway, so framed to please,
    Should ever from usurper meet controul!   20
That ever shrivell'd wealth, or gray disease,
    Should mar the grateful concord of the soul!
    That bloated sediment of crazing bowl
Should crop thy blossoms which untasted die!
    Or that the blistering phrase of babbler foul   25
Should e'er profane thy altars, framed to lie
Veil'd from all heaven and earth, save silent Fancy's eye!

4.

O I will worship even before thy bust,
   When my dimm'd eye no more thy smile can see!
While this deserted bosom beats, it must   30
    Still beat in unison with hope and thee!
    For I have wept o'er perish'd ecstasy,
And o'er the fall of beauty's early prime!
    But I will dream of new delights to be,
When moon and stars have ceased their range sublime, 35
And angels rung the knell of all-consuming Time!

5.

Then speed, thou great coeval of the sun;
   Thy world with flowers and snows alternate sow!
Long has thy whelming tide resistless run,
    And swell'd the seas of wickedness and woe!   40
    While moons shall wane, and mundane oceans flow,
To count the hours of thy dominion o'er,
    The dyes of human guilt shall deeper grow,
And millions sink to see thy reign no more!
Haste, haste thy guilty course to yon eternal shore!   45

6.

Cease, thou wild Muse, thy vague unbodied lay!
   What boots these wanderings from thy onward tale?
I know thee well! when once thou fliest astray,
    To lure thee back no soothing can avail.
    Thou lovest amid the burning stars to sail,   50
Or sing with sea-maids down the coral deep;
    The groves of visionary worlds to hail,
In moonlight dells thy fairy rites to keep,
Or through the wilderness on booming pinion sweep.

7.

Wilt thou not stoop, where beauty sits forlorn,   55
   Trembling at symptoms of approaching woe?
Where lovely Ila, by the aged thorn,
    Notes what she scarce dare trust her heart to know?
    Mark how her cheek's new roses come and go—
Has Mador dared his virtuous vow to break?   60
    It cannot be!—we may not deem it so!
Spare the ungrateful thought, for mercy's sake!
Alas! man still is man—And woman!—ah! how weak!

8.

Why do the maidens of the strath rejoice,
    And lilt with meaning gesture on the loan? 65
Why do they smirk, and talk with giggling voice
    Of laces, and of stays; and thereupon
    Hang many a fruitful jest?—Ah! is there none
The truth to pledge, and prove the nuptial vow?
    Alas! the Friar on pilgrimage is gone; 70
Mador is lost—none else the secret knew,
And all is deem'd pretext assumptive and untrue.

9.

Slander prevails! to woman's longing mind
    Sweet as the April blossom to the bee;
Her meal that never palls, but leaves behind 75
    An appetite still yearning food to see:
    Kincraigy's dame of perspicacity
Sees nought at all amiss, but flounces on;
    Her brawling humour shows increased to be;
Much does she speak, in loud and grumbling tone, 80
Nor time takes to reflect, nor even a prayer to con.

10.

The injured Albert timely sent command
    That pierced Kincraigy to the inmost soul,
To drive his worthless daughter from the land,
    Or forthwith yield, of goods and gear, the whole. 85
    Alternative severe!—no tale of dole
The chief would hear, on full revenge intent.
    The good sagacious dame, in murmuring growl,
Proposed to drive her forth incontinent,
For she deserved it all, and Albert might relent. 90

11.

"She is to blame," Kincraigy made reply,
    "And may deserve so hard a guerdon well;
But so dost thou, and haply I may try
    That last expedient with a shrew so fell;
    But when I do, no man shall me compel: 95
For thy own good, to poverty I yield;
    My child is still my own, and shall not tell
At Heaven's high bar, that I, her only shield,
For blame that was not hers, expell'd her to the field."

12.

Kincraigy leaves his ancient home with tears,   100
   And sits in lowly cot without a name;
No angry word from him his daughter hears,
   But Oh! how pined the much-degraded dame!
   Plaint follow'd plaint, and blame was eked to blame.
Her muster-roll of grievances how long!   105
   She mentions not her darling Minstrel's fame,
His spotless honour, nor affection strong,
But to her weeping child imputes each grievous wrong.

13.

Conceal'd within the cot's sequester'd nook,
   Where fire had never beam'd the gloom to cheer,   110
Young Ila Moore is doom'd her woes to brook,
   And every query's answer'd by a tear.
What mean those tiny robes, conceal'd with fear?
These clothes, dear Maid, are all unmeet for thee!
   Are all unfitting human thing to wear,   115
Save noble infant on his nurse's knee,
Yet them thou dost survey, and weep when none can see.

14.

O Maiden of the bright and melting eye,
   Of the soft velvet cheek and balmy breath,
Whose lips the coral's deepest tints outvie,   120
   Thy bosom fairer than the winter wreath!
   Before thou yield'st those lips of simple faith,
Or givest that heaving breast to love's caress,
   O look beyond!—the sweet luxuriant path
May lead thee into lab'rinth of distress!   125
Think of this comely May, nor deem thy danger less.

15.

Blame not the bard, who yearns thy peace to save,
   Who fain would see thy virtuous worth excel
Thy beauty, and thy purity engrave
   Where time may scarce the lines of life cancel.   130
   Deem not he on thy foibles lists to dwell,
Thy failings, or the dangers thee belay;
   'Tis all to caution thee, and warn thee well.
Wipe but thy little stains of love away,
And thou art goodness all, and pure as bloom of May.   135

16.

To give thy secret ear to lover's tale,
   Or cast approving glance, is kindly done;
But, ere thy soul the darling sweets inhale,
   Mark out the bourn—nor farther be thou won.
   Eventful is the sequel, once begun,   140
And all delusive sweets that onward lie.
   Think of the inmost nook of cottage lone,
Of the blench'd cheek, the blear'd and swimming eye,
And how 'twill thee become, th' unsainted lullaby!

17.

'Tis done! and Shame his masterpiece hath wrought!   145
   Why should the laws of God and man combine
To sear the heart with keenest sorrows fraught,
   And every blush and every tear enshrine
   In brazen tomb of punishment malign?
The gentle sufferer beacon stands to scorn!   150
   Kincraigy's dame is sunk in woes condign!
A helpless minstrel to her house is born!
A grandson, hale and fair, and comely as the morn.

18.

Poor child of shame! thy fortune to divine
   Would conjure up the scenes of future pain!   155
No father's house, nor shielding arm is thine!
   No banquet hails thee, stranger of disdain!
   A lowly shelter from the wind and rain
Hides thy young weetless head, unwelcome guest!
   And thy unholy frame must long remain   160
Unhousell'd, and by churchman's tongue unblest!
Yet peaceful is thy sleep, cradled on guileless breast!

19.

Hard works Kincraigy mid his woodland reign,
   And boasts his earnings to his fluster'd dame;
Seem'd as unknowing the event of pain,   165
   Nor once by him is named his daughter's name,
   Till ardent matron of the hamlet came,
And brought the child abrupt his eye before.
   He saw the guiltless his protection claim,
With little arms outstretch'd seem'd to implore—   170
He kiss'd the babe and wept, then hasted to the door.

20.

But O Kincraigy's dame is warp'd in dread!
   The days of Heaven's forbearance are outgone,
And round th' unchristen'd babe's unholy bed
   No guardian spirits watch at midnight lone!   175
   Well to malignant elves the same was known—
There slept the babe, to them an easy prey.
   O! every nightly buzz or distant moan
Drove the poor dame's unrooted wits away!
Her terror 'twas by night, her thought and prayer by day.   180

21.

Still wax'd her dread, for ah! too well she knew
   Her floor, o'ernight, had frames unearthly borne!
Around her cot the giggling fairies flew,
   And all arrangement alter'd ere the morn!
   At eve, the candle of its beams was shorn,   185
While a blue halo round the flame would play;
   And she could hear the fairies' fitful horn
Ring in her ears an eldrich roundelay,
When every eye was shut, and her's all wakeful lay.

22.

And many a private mark the infant bore,   190
   Survey'd each morn with dread which none can tell,
Lest the real child was borne to downward shore,
   And in his stead, and form, by fairy spell,
   Some froward elfin child, deform'd and fell!
O how her troubled breast with horror shook,   195
   Lest thing from confines of the lower hell
Might sit upon her knee and on her look!
'Twas more than her weak mind and fading form could brook.

23.

Sweet Ila Moore had borne the world's revile
   With meekness, and with warm repentant tears;   200
At church-anathemas she well could smile,
   And silent oft of faithless man she hears.
   But now a kind misjudging parent's fears
Opprest her heart—her father too would sigh
   O'er the unrighteous babe, whose early years   205
Excluded were from saints' society!
Disown'd by God and man, an heathen he might die!

24.

Forthwith she tried a letter to indite,
　　To rouse the faithless Mador's dormant flame:
Her soul was rack'd with feelings opposite;   210
　　She found no words proportion'd to his blame.
　　At memory's page her blushes went and came;
And aye she stoop'd and o'er the cradle hung,
　　Call'd her loved infant by his father's name,
Then framed a little lay, and thus she sung—   215
"Thy father's far away, thy mother all too young!

25.

"Be still, my babe! be still!—the die is cast!
　　Beyond thy weal no joy remains for me!
Thy mother's spring was clouded and o'erpast
　　Erewhile the blossom open'd on the tree!   220
　　But I will nurse thee kindly on my knee,
In spite of every taunt and jeering tongue;
　　O thy sweet eye will melt my wrongs to see!
And thy kind little heart with grief be wrung!
Thy father's far away, thy mother all too young!   225

26.

"If haggard poverty should overtake,
　　And threat our onward journey to forelay,
For thee I'll pull the berries of the brake,
　　Wake half the night, and toil the live-long day;
　　And when proud manhood o'er thy brow shall play,   230
For me thy bow in forest shall be strung.
　　The memory of my errors shall decay,
And of the song of shame I oft have sung,
Of father far away, and mother all too young!

27.

"But O! when mellow'd lustre gilds thine eye,   235
　　And love's soft passion thrills thy youthful frame,
Let this memorial bear thy mind on high
　　Above the guilty and regretful flame,
　　The mildew of the soul, the mark of shame!
Think of the fruit before the bloom that sprung!   240
　　When in the twilight bower with beauteous dame,
Let this unbreathed lay hang on thy tongue—
Thy father's far away, thy mother all too young!"

28.

When days and nights a stained scroll had seen
   Beneath young Ila Moore's betrothed eye;   245
When many a tear had dropt the lines between,
   When dim the page with many a burning sigh,
   A boy is charged to Scotland's court to hie
The pledge to bear, nor leave the Minstrel's door
   Till answer came.—Alas! nor low, nor high,   250
Porter nor groom, nor warder of the tower,
Had ever heard the name of Mador of the Moor.

Mador of the Moor

Canto Fourth

The Palmer

Argument

Did ye never hear o' the puir auld man,
That doughtna live, and coudna die?
Wha spak to the spirits a' night lang,
An' saw the things we coudna see,
An' raised the bairnies out o' the grave?—
O but a waesome sight was he!

Mador of the Moor

Canto Fourth

The Palmer

1.

THERE is a bounded sphere, where human grief
  May all the energies of mind benumb;
'Twixt purpose and regret, it seeks relief
  In unavailing plaint, or musings dumb;
  But to o'erwhelming height when mounts the sum,   5
Oft, to itself superior, mind hath shone.
  That broken reed, Dependence, overcome,
Where dwells the might that may the soul unthrone,
Whose proud resolve is moor'd on its own powers alone?

2.

Why is young Ila dight in robes so gay,   10
  Her hue more lovely than the gold refined?
Why bears she to the southern vales away,
  And leaves the woody banks of Tay behind,
  Her beauteous boy well wrapt from sun and wind
In mantle spangled like the heath in flower?—   15
  Ah! she is gone her wandering love to find,
In court or camp, in hall or lady's bower,
Resolved to die, or find young Mador of the Moor.

3.

Had she not cause to weep her piteous plight?
  In the wide world unfriended thus to be!   20
A babe, unwean'd, companion of her flight!—
  She did not weep; her spirits bounded free,
  And, all indignant that her injury
Moved no congenial feeling on her side,
  With robe of green, upfolded to her knee,   25
And light unsandall'd foot, o'er wastes so wide
She journey'd far away, with Heaven alone to guide.

4.

She had not traversed far the woods of Bran,
   Nor of her native hills had lost the view,
Where oft, on maidhood's lightsome foot, she ran,   30
   Pilf'ring the rock-rose and the harebell blue,
   Or moorland berries bathed in autumn dew,
When, startled, she beheld a Palmer gray
   Rise from beneath a lonely ronkled yew,
Where he had prostrate lain since dawn of day,   35
Who proffer'd her his hand, companion of her way.

5.

He seem'd familiar with her wrongs and aim!
   Full oft she view'd his face, if she might see
Some feature there that might acquaintance claim—
   It wore the mysteries of eternity!   40
   That face was mild as face of age could be,
Yet something there 'twas dread to look upon!
   A mien between profound and vacancy,
Bewraying thought to mortal man unknown,
Or soul abstract from sense, with feelings all its own.   45

6.

She marvell'd much to hear, as on they went,
   His heavenly converse and his sage replies;
But mark'd him oft regard with fond intent
   Things all invisible to mortal eyes.
   The light-wing'd winds, that flaunted thro' the skies,   50
Spoke in small voices, like the Elfin's tongue;
   From welling fountains harmonies would rise,
Like song of lark high in the rainbow hung;
Seem'd as if distant hymns of other worlds they sung.

7.

In pleasing dread she sojourn'd by his side,   55
   Nor durst she his companionship forego;
But either fear her faculties belied,
   Else speech was whisper'd from the earth below,
   And elemental converse round did flow:
The stranger answer'd oft in varied tone;   60
   Then he would smile, and chide she knew not who!
Seem'd as to him each herald cloud was known,
That crept along the hill, or sail'd the starry zone.

8.

"Give me thy child, fair dame," he said, and smiled,
   Clasping his arms around the comely boy.   65
"Give me the child, thy youth is sorely toil'd,
   And I will bear him half the way with joy."
  She loosed her hold, unwilling to seem coy:
Scarce was the timid act of sufferance done,
   Ere wild ideas wrought her sore annoy,   70
That Elfin King th' unchristen'd babe had won:
Deep in her heart she pray'd that God would save her son!

9.

She look'd each moment when the old man's form
   Would change to something of unearthly guise;
She look'd each moment when the thunder-storm   75
   Would roll in folded sulphur from the skies,
   And snatch them from her terror-darken'd eyes!
She follow'd nigh, enfeebled with affright,
   And saw her boy, in roguish playful wise,
Pulling the old man's beard with all his might,—   80
The change to him was fraught with new and high delight.

10.

Her heart was quieted, but ill at rest,
   And gave unwonted thoughts a teeming birth
Of this most reverend and mysterious guest,
   Who scarcely seem'd an habitant of earth.   85
   The day was wearing late, no friendly hearth
Was nigh, where converse might the time betray;
   The storm was hanging on the mountain swarth
Condense and gloomy, threatening sore dismay
To wanderer of the hills, on rough and pathless way.   90

11.

A darksome shieling, westward on the waste,
   Stood like a lonely hermit of the glen;
A small green sward its bastion'd walls embraced,
   Kything right simply sweet to human ken:
   On tiny path, unmark'd by steps of men,   95
To that they turn'd, in hopes of welcome meet;
   'Twas only then the grovelling badger's den,
Damp was its floor, untrode by human feet,
And cold, cold lay the hearth, uncheer'd by kindly heat!

12.

The marten, from his vault beneath the wall,   100
   Peep'd forth with fiend-like eye and fetid breath;
They heard the young brock's whining hunger-call,
   And the grim pole-cat's grinding voice beneath.
   The merlin, from his rafter'd home, in wrath,
Flitted with flapping wing and erdlich scream;   105
   No downward sepulchre, nor vault of death,
Did ever deed of horror more beseem;
'Twas like some rueful cave seen in perturbed dream.

13.

The storm was on, and darkening still behind;
   Alternate rush'd the rain and rattling hail;   110
In deepen'd breathings sigh'd the cumber'd wind;
   Play'd the swift gleam along the boreal-pale,
   While distant thunder murmur'd o'er the gale;
Far up th' incumbent cloud its voice began,
   Then, like resistless angel, bound to scale   115
The southern heaven, along the void it ran,
Booming, in wrathful tone, vengeance on sinful man.

14.

It was a dismal and portentous hour:
   A mute astonishment and torpid dread
Had settled on the soul of Ila Moore;   120
   In whisper'd prayers, of Heaven she sought remede;
   For well she knew, that He, who deign'd to feed
The plumeless sea-bird on the stormy main,
   The raven, and the osprey's orphan breed,
To save an injured heart would not disdain,   125
Nor leave the souls he made to sorrow and to pain.

15.

Nigh and more nigh the rolling thunder came,
   Muffled in moving pall of midnight hue;
Fiercer and fiercer burst the flakes of flame
   From out the forge of Heaven in burning blue.   130
   They split the yawning cloud, and downward flew,
Before their wrath the solid hill was riven;
   Some in the lake their fiery heads imbrue,
Its startled waters to the sky were driven,
Belching as if it mock'd the angry coil of Heaven.   135

16.

O ye, who mock religion's faded sway,
  And flout the mind that bows to Heaven's decree,
Think of the fortitude of that fair May,
  Her simple youth, in such a place to be,
  In such a night, and in such company,—   140
With guest she ween'd not man of woman born,
  A babe unblest upon her youthful knee!
Had she not cause to deem her case forlorn?
No! Trusting to her God, she calmly waited morn.

17.

The Palmer did no sign of fear bewray,   145
  But raised a fire with well-accustom'd hand,
Smiled at the thunder's break and startling bray,
  The chilly hail-shower and the whizzing brand,
  In wild turmoil that vollied o'er the land.
Then he would mutter prayer, or rite of sin;   150
  Then prattle to the child in language bland;
While the fond mother groan'd in heart within,
Lest at the turn of night the fiends her babe might win.

18.

The Palmer, for his helpless partners, made
  A bed of flowery heath and rushes green;   155
Then o'er the twain his mantle kindly spread,
  And bade them sleep secure, though lodged so mean;
  For near that lowly couch, by them unseen,
There stood a form, familiar to his eye,
  Whose look was mark'd with dignity serene,   160
To ward the freakish fays that linger'd nigh,
Who seem'd on evil bent—he saw not, knew not why.

19.

The Palmer watch'd beside the hissing flame,
  The mother clasp'd her child in silence deep;
That speech of mystery thrill'd her ardent frame,   165
  For why?—she knew the fays their wake did keep
  To reave her child if she should yield to sleep!
No sleep she knew—if woman's word is aught—
  But, venturing o'er her coverlet to peep,
Whether through glamour or bewilder'd thought,   170
She there beheld a scene with awful wonder fraught.

20.

From every crevice of the wall there look'd
  Small elvish faces of malignity!
And O! their gleaming eyes could ill be brook'd!
  All bent upon the babe that slumber'd by!   175
  Ready they seem'd upon their prey to fly,
And oft they sprung, or stole with wary tread;
  But o'er the couch a form of majesty
Stood all serene, whose eye the spirits fled,
Waring the golden wand she waved around the bed.   180

21.

The Palmer saw—and, as the damsel thought,
  Joy'd that th' assailing spirits were outdone:
Still wax'd their number, still they fiercer fought,
  Till the last lingering sand of night was run,
  Till the red star the gate of Heaven had won,   185
And woke the dreaming eagle's lordly bay,
  And heath-cock's larum on the moorland dun;
Then did they shrink, and vanish from the fray,
Far from the eye of Morn, on downward paths away.

22.

Spent was the night, and the old reverend sire   190
  Had never closed his eyes, but watch'd and wept,
Muttering low vespers o'er his feeble fire,
  Or, all intent, a watchful silence kept.
  Now o'er his silver beard the round tear dripp'd,
Aside his cowl with hurried hand he flung,   195
  Wiped his high brow, and cheek with sorrow steep'd,
Then, with an upcast eye and tremulous tongue,
Unto the God of Life this matin hymn he sung.

The Palmer's Morning Hymn

Lauded be thy name for ever,
Thou, of life the guard and giver!   200
Thou canst guard thy creatures sleeping,
Heal the heart long broke with weeping,
Rule the ouphes and elves at will

That vex the air or haunt the hill,
And all the fury subject keep 205
Of boiling cloud and chafed deep!
I have seen, and well I know it!
Thou hast done, and Thou wilt do it!
God of stillness and of motion!
Of the rainbow and the ocean! 210
Of the mountain, rock, and river!
Blessed be Thy name for ever!

I have seen Thy wond'rous might
Through the shadows of this night!
Thou, who slumber'st not, nor sleepest! 215
Blest are they Thou kindly keepest!
Spirits, from the ocean under,
Liquid flame, and levell'd thunder,
Need not waken nor alarm them—
All combined they cannot harm them. 220
God of evening's yellow ray;
God of yonder dawning day,
That rises from the distant sea
Like breathings of eternity!
Thine the flaming sphere of light! 225
Thine the darkness of the night!
Thine are all the gems of even,
God of angels! God of heaven!
God of life, that fade shall never!
Glory to Thy name for ever! 230

23.

That little song of rapt devotion fell
   Upon a feeling heart, to nature true,
So soothing sweet, 'twas like the distant swell
   Of seraph hymn along the vales of blue,
   When first they ope to sainted spirit's view, 235
That through the wilds of space hath journey'd far,
   Hoping, yet trembling as he onward flew,
Lest God the emerald gates of Heaven might bar,
Till rests the joyous shade on some sweet peaceful star.

24.

Till then she knew not that the wonderous sage   240
   Was conversant with Heaven, or fiends of hell;
Till then she knew not that his reverend age
   Cared of th' Almighty or his love to tell.
   Sweet and untroubled as the dews that fell
Her morning slumbers were—the Palmer lay   245
   Stretch'd on the unyielding stone, accustom'd well
To penance dire, and spirits' wild deray:
There slept they all in peace till high uprose the day.

25.

They journey'd on by Almond's silver stream,
   That wimpled down a green untrodden wild;   250
By turns their hapless stories were the theme,
   And aye the listener bore the pleased child.
   The attentive sage nor chided nor reviled,
When simple tale of maiden love she said;
   Meek his reproof, and flow'd in words so mild,   255
It tended much her constancy to aid,
And cheer her guileless heart from truth that never stray'd.

26.

"Fair dame," he said, "thou may'st have done amiss;
   And thou art brought to poverty and woe!
What now remains, but quietly to kiss   260
   The lash that hangs o'er virtue's overthrow?
   Be virtue still thy meed, thy trust, and know
It thee befits from murmur to refrain.
   No plaint of thy just wounds be heard to flow,
The hand that gave will bind them up again.   265
List my distracting tale, and blame thy fortune then!

27.

"I was the lord of Stormont's fertile bound,
   Of Isla's vale, and Eroch's woodland glade.
I loved—I sigh'd—my warmest hopes were crown'd—
   O deed of shame! I vow'd and I betray'd!   270
   The proud Matilda, now no longer maid,
Disdain'd my base unfaithful heart to move;
   She knew not to solicit, nor upbraid;
But did a deed, the last of lawless love!
Ah! it hath sear'd my soul, that peace no more shall prove!

28.

"I knew not all, yet marvell'd much to see
   That scarce a circling year had roll'd away,
Ere she appear'd the gayest maid to be
   That graced the hall, or gambol'd at the play.
   With Methven's lord was fix'd her bridal day: 280
Proud of her triumph, I—the chiefest guest—
   Led her to church—Ah! never such array
Did woman's form of vanity invest!
Bright as the orient ray, or streamer of the west.

29.

"Scarce had we stepp'd, the foremost of the train,   285
   Within the church-yard's low and crumbling wall,
When, sweet as sun-beam gleaming through the rain,
   We saw a shining row of children small.
   Fair were their forms, and fair their robes withal;
But O! each radiant and unmoving eye   290
   Was fix'd on us!—forget I never shall
How well they seem'd my very soul to spy!
And hers—the sparkling bride, that moved so graceful by!

30.

"Proud of their note, or charmed with the sight,
   She turn'd aside with step of dignity: 295
All still and motionless, they stood upright,
   Save one sweet babe that slightly bent the knee,
   With such a smile of mild benignity!
These eyes shall ne'er such face again behold!
   His flaxen curls like filmy silk did flee;   300
His tiny form seem'd cast in heavenly mould;
His cheek like blossom pale, in April morning cold.

31.

" 'Sweet babe,' she simper'd, with affected mien,
   'Thou art a lovely boy; if thou wert mine,
I'd deck thee in the gold and diamonds sheen,   305
   And daily bathe thee in the rosy wine;
   The musk-rose and the balmy eglantine
Around thy soft and silken couch should play;
   How fondly would these arms around thee twine!
Asleep or waking, I would watch thee aye,   310
Caress thee all the night, and love thee all the day.'

32.

" 'O lady, of the proud unfeeling soul,
　　'Tis not three little months since I was thine;
And thou did'st deck me in the grave-cloth foul,
　　And bathe me in the blood—that blood was mine!   315
　　Instead of damask rose and eglantine,
The reptile's brood plays round my guiltless core!
　　Ah! could'st thou deem there was no eye divine,
And that the deed would sleep for evermore?
Did'st thou ne'er see this pale, this pleading look before?'   320

33.

"That moment I beheld, beneath mine eye,
　　A smiling babe, with hands and eyes upraised;
A pale and frantic mother trembled nigh—
　　She kneel'd—she seized its arm!—the knife was raised—
　　'Hold, hold!' I cried; yet motionless I gazed,   325
And saw——O God of Heaven! I see it now!
　　I see the eye-beam sink in deadly haze;
The quivering lip, the bent and gelid brow!—
O I shall see that sight in being yet to know!

34.

"To wild disorder turn'd the bridal hall!   330
　　O still at me her frenzied looks she threw!
All in amazement fled the festival,
　　The sufferer to the wild at midnight flew!—
　　Thou found'st me underneath a lonely yew;
There I have pray'd, and oft must pray again!   335
　　There ravens fed! and red the daisies grew!—
Yet *they* were white! without a dye or stain,
The slender scatter'd bones there bleached in the rain!

35.

"Fair dame, thy crime is purity to mine!
　　I must go pray, for I am haunted still!   340
In Heaven is mercy!—I may not repine,
　　But bow submissive, since it is the will
　　Of Him, who cares and feels for human ill!
They deem me mad, and laugh my woes to scorn,
　　And name me crazy Connel of the hill: 345
My heart is broke! my brain with watching worn!
I must go pray to God, for I am rack'd and torn!"

36.

He kneel'd beside the grey stone on the heath,
 And loud his orisons of dread began;
Such words were never framed of human breath,   350
 Such tones of vehemence never pour'd by man!
 Madly through vailed mysteries he ran,
With voice of howling and unvision'd eye;
 Then would the tears drop o'er his cheek so wan,
And he would calmly plead, with throb and sigh,   355
And name his Saviour's name with deep humility.

37.

Three days they journey'd on through moor and dale,
 Till faded far the hills of Tay behind;
Still he was gentle as the southern gale,
 Mild as the lamb, compassionate and kind!   360
 But O far wilder than the winter wind
Whene'er a world of spirits was the theme!
 Then he would name unbodied things of mind,
That paced the air, or skimm'd along the stream!
His life seem'd all a waste, a wild and troubled dream.   365

38.

Still had the crime of innocence betray'd,
 Which terminated not with shame alone,
Oppress'd his heart and on his reason prey'd;
 In tears of blood that crime he did bemoan.
 Though mazed were all his thoughts, yet to atone   370
For that to Heaven which reckless he had done,
 O'er maiden innocence to watch anon
He ceased not, wearied not, till life was run.
O be his tale a warning, youthful vice to shun!

39.

When nigh the verge of southern vale they came,   375
 And green Strathallan open'd to their view,
He blest the child and mother, in the name
 Of heaven's Eternal King, with reverence due;
 Then turning round, with madden'd strides withdrew
Back to his desart solitude again,   380
 To watch the moon, and pray beneath his yew,
Controlling spirits on their mountain reign,
Till death brought unity, for ever to remain.

Mador of the Moor

Canto Fifth

The Christening

Argument

I gat ye in my father's bower
  Wi' muckle shame and sin,
An' brought thee up in good green wood
  Aneath the heavy rain.
Oft ha'e I by thy cradle sat,
  An' fondly seen thee sleep—

    *   *   *   *
    *   *   *   *

Gae rowe my young son in the silk,
An' lay my lady as white as the milk.

Mador of the Moor
Canto Fifth

The Christening

1.

OLD Strevline, thou stand'st beauteous on the height,
  Amid thy peaceful vales of every dye,
Amid bewilder'd waves of silvery light
  That maze the mind and toil the raptured eye;
  Thy distant mountains spiring to the sky,   5
Seem blended with the mansions of the blest;
  How proudly rise their gilded points on high
Above the morning cloud and man's behest!
Like thrones of angels hung upon the welkin's breast.

2.

For these I love thee! but I love thee more   10
  For the gray relics of thy martial towers,
Thy mouldering palaces and ramparts hoar,
  Throned on the granite pile that grimly lours,
  Memorial of the times, when hostile powers
So often proved thy stedfast patriot worth.   15
  May every honour wait thy future hours,
And glad the children of thy kindred Forth!
I love thy very name, old bulwark of the North!

3.

Alas! the winding Forth, and golden vale,
  Caught not the eye of her who sought thy gate!   20
Her spirits sunk, her heart began to fail!
  Weeping she came, nor could her tale relate;
  Mador she named, and, trembling for her fate,
Watch'd the tall porter's dark unmeaning stare,
  Who jested rudely of her hapless state,   25
And bade her to some distant country fare,
For such a name as that no Scot did ever bear.

4.

Humbly she begg'd to fare the porch within,
   That of the nobles she a view might gain,
And her enquiries cautiously begin;   30
    But all her urgent prayers and tears were vain.
    Harsh she was told, "no longer to remain,
For knights and lords would soon be passing by,
    And they would be offended at such stain
Upon their knighthood and their honours high: 35
That such as she seem'd made for mischief purposely."

5.

No beam of anger ray'd her glistening eye,
   It sunk like star within the rubied west;
Or like the tinted dew-bell, seen to lie
    Upon the rose-leaf tremblingly at rest,   40
    Then softly sinks upon its opening breast—
So sunk her eye, while firmly she replied,
    "Since no appeal, nor plea of the distress'd,
To Scotland's court may come, whate'er betide,
Thou shalt not drive me hence till I am satisfied."   45

6.

O many an eve she wander'd round the rock,
   In hopes her faithless Minstrel to espy;
And many a time to dame and townsman spoke,
    With blush obtrusive, and with question shy;
    But nor by name, by garb, by minstrelsy,   50
Nor strict discernment, could she Mador find.
    Her fond and ardent hopes began to die!
In cheerless apathy with all mankind,
She only wish'd to leave the world and shame behind!

7.

Loth to depart and seek a cheerless home,   55
   Down at the base of Strevline's rock she lay;
She wish'd her head laid in the peaceful tomb!
    She kiss'd her boy, but word she could not say.
    She turn'd her eyes to heaven in act to pray—
O hold those lips, unused to give offence!   60
    That prayer will rise in wild impassion'd way,
How have thy woes arisen, and from whence?
O search, before thou darest accuse Omnipotence!

8.

The worthy Abbot of Dunfermline came,
  He mark'd her beauty, and he heard her weep. 65
Silent he paused, and eyed her lovely frame;
  For churchmen aye observant eye do keep
  On female beauty, though devotion deep
And homilies behove the holy mood;
  From rostrum still in wily guise they peep— 70
For why?—by them 'tis wisely understood,
That to admire the chief of all Heaven's works is good.

9.

The Abbot ne'er had look'd on face so meek!
  The pleasure that it gave was mix'd with pain;
He saw her lift her full blue eyes to speak, 75
  She only sigh'd and cast them down again,
  Then view'd her babe, while tears fell down like rain,
Wiped her young cheek, and back her ringlets threw.
  The Abbot's honest bosom heaved amain!
A look so lovely ne'er had met his view! 80
'Twas like a forest rose, wet with untimely dew!

10.

Question respectful, and sincere reply,
  Brought on a long and earnest conference;
The tale was told of Mador's perfidy
  Which thou hast heard—but still, on some pretence 85
  Of treacherous memory, or lost incidence,
The Abbot caused her tell it o'er and o'er;
  Then did he stand in long and deep suspense,
As bent some dubious mystery to explore;
As one who little said, but thought and knew much more. 90

11.

Still did his eye oppress the gentle dame;
  Not on her face, but arm, it seem'd to stay;
She ween'd her boy did this attention claim,
  And set his cap, and don'd his overlay;
  Then watch'd the Abbot's eye—but not that way 95
It seem'd to bend—A trivial ring she wore,
  Of silver framed, neglected, old, and gray,
Warp'd with the unknown mysteries of yore;
'Twas on that ancient ring his eye directly bore.

12.

"Fair dame," he said, "did thy betrayer leave   100
   No token of his faith, nor pledge of love?
Did he, like knight, no ring or bracelet give,
    Which he was bound to challenge or approve?"
    Her thought-bewilder'd eyes began to move
Now to the ring, now to the Abbot's face;   105
   Faint recollections o'er their lustre wove
A still, a doubtful, melancholy grace—
'Twas like an April sky, which dubious shades embrace.

13.

She spread her fair hand trembling in the air—
   "Save that old ring, no other pledge have I;   110
He gave't in moment of distracting care,
    When from my arms and danger forced to fly:
    Something he said, but of what tendency,
Or what effect, remembrance ne'er could frame.
    From the device I nothing may imply,   115
Nor mark it bears, unless the moulder's name;
Small its avail to me, nor other pledge I claim."

14.

A glow of anger flush'd the Abbot's face;
   He knew the old disvalued ring full well;
And much its owner wish'd he to disgrace,   120
    For he was generous, but shrewdly fell.
    "I'll find him out," he said, "by search or spell,
If in fair Scotland he holds rank or place;
    Remain thou here till I our Sovereign tell."
Then up the hill he strode with hurried pace,   125
And left the lovely dame in sad uncertain case.

15.

Scarce was he gone, when on the path she saw,
   That leads from vale of Strevline to the town,
A weary wight that toward her did draw,
    With hanging hose, and plaid around him thrown;   130
    His grizzled locks waved o'er his cheek so brown;
She thought his stoop and stride too well she knew!
    His mournful eyes to earth were fixed down,
Save when a transient glance he upward threw
Where Scotland's palace rose, and her broad banners flew.

16.

She heard him mutter vow of fell revenge!
  Closer to earth she clung, in fear and shame,
Resolved nor word nor look with him to change;
  But all unbrookable as nigh he came
  Her bosom yearn'd, her heart was in a flame.   140
Feebly she cried, "My father, turn this way!"
  Up stretch'd the stranger's rough uncourtly frame—
'Twas old Kincraigy, from the banks of Tay,
Who stood like statue grim, in wild and doubtful way!

17.

That painful greeting may not be defined;   145
  Nature's own language flow'd from either tongue;
Nor fell reproach, nor countenance unkind,
  With freezing scowl, above their soothings hung:
  Both child and mother to his bosom clung;
He wiped her tears, and bade from grief refrain;   150
  "Thou art my child, and thou hast suffer'd wrong.
How could'st thou leave me, prey to sharpest pain?
But I have found thee now, we ne'er shall part again!"

18.

Straight to the royal hall the Abbot went,
  Where sat the King, his dames, and nobles all;   155
Scarce did he beckon, scarce his brow he bent,
  But raised his hand their sole regard to call,
  And thus began, while silence sway'd the hall:—
"My Liege, I grieve such message here to bring;
  But now there waits below your palace wall   160
The loveliest flower that ever graced the spring,
That ever mounted throne, or shone in courtly ring.

19.

"She bears a form of such delightful mould,
  I ween'd before me sylvan goddess stood.
Such beauty these old eyes did ne'er behold!   165
  —Nay, smile not, dames—for, by the blessed rood,
  That I aver I pledge me to make good.
She's Beauty's self pourtray'd, and to her breast
  Is prest a lovely babe of playful mood.
She has been wrong'd, betray'd, and sore oppress'd,   170
And, could a heart believe!—the traitor here is guest."

20.

The King was wroth, and rose from off his throne,
  Look'd round for flush of guilt, then raised his hand:
"By this!" said he, "the knight that so hath done
  Shall reparation make, or quit the land.   175
  I hold not light the crime, and do command
A full relation—He who can betray
  Such beauty, with false vow, and promise bland,
As lieve will dupe his king in treacherous way.
The ruthless traitor's name, and hers, good Abbot, say." 180

21.

"Thou art my generous King!" the Abbot cried,
  "And Heaven will bless thee for this just award!
This feeble arm of mine hath erst been tried,
  And for the injured has a foeman dared;
  And should the knight your mandate disregard,—   185
'Tis old and nerveless now, and small its power,
  But all his skill its vengeance shall not ward—
Beshrew his heart, but he shall rue the hour!—
The knight is Mador hight, the dame fair Ila Moore."

22.

As ever you saw the chambers of the west,   190
  When summer suns had journey'd to the main,
Now sallow pale, now momently oppress'd
  With crimson flush, the prelude of the rain,
  So look'd the King; and stamp'd and scowl'd amain,
To stay the Abbot's speech, who deign'd no heed,   195
  But did, with sharpest acritude, arraign
The low deceit, the doer and the deed,
And lauded much the King for that he had decreed.

23.

"I think I know the wight," the King replied;
  "He is abash'd, and will not own it now;   200
But my adjudgment shall be ratified,—
  A King hath vow'd, and must not break his vow."
  Then look'd he round, with smooth deceitful brow,
As he the mark of conscious guilt had seen;
  Then, with majestic air and motion slow,   205
Walk'd with the Abbot forth into the green;
But all unknown the strain of converse them between.

24.

The Abbot hasted to his lovely ward—
  Judge of his false conjecture and alarms,
When he beheld this nymph of high regard 210
  So fondly folded in a stranger's arms.
  But O how much they added to her charms,
The filial tears adown her cheek that ran!
  The kindest glow the human heart that warms
Play'd o'er the visage of the holy man; 215
While he, to sooth his guests, an artful tale began.

25.

He led them to his home of peace the while,
  Where all was rich, yet all in simple guise,
And strove with cheerful converse to beguile
  Each latent fear and sorrowful surmise. 220
  Well skill'd to read, in language of the eyes,
What the still workings of the heart might be,
  He bade her don those robes of courtly guise,
For they were hers, a gift bestowed free,
And ere the fall of night her Minstrel she might see. 225

26.

When from the chamber she return'd, array'd
  In braided silk and rich embroidery,
The Abbot rose, confounded and dismay'd,
  And old Kincraigy nigh had bent his knee.
  An earthly form she scarcely seem'd to be, 230
Such dazzling beauty neither once had seen.
  "Fair dame, a lady thou may'st shortly be,"
Said the good Abbot, with enraptured mien,
"But Nature meant thee more, she form'd thee for a queen!"

27.

Scarce had she answer with a blush assay'd, 235
  Scarce raised th' astonish'd babe unto her breast,
When enter'd Mador, with a look that said
  His heart was generous, and his mind oppress'd.
  His minstrel garb he wore, and purple crest—
Nought of his woodland flower he could espy! 240
  But one who on a silken couch did rest,
That seem'd some form of eastern deity!
The Minstrel bow'd full low, while wonder dimm'd his eye.

28.

The shifting hues that sported o'er her face
  Were like the streamers of the rosy eve,   245
And to her beauty lent a nameless grace—
  Those blushes could not Mador undeceive!
  His fancy made no motion to believe
That e'er his highland maid had half the charms,
  Till the good Abbot did his mind relieve,   250
In pity of a female's fond alarms.
"What, my first love!" he cried, and sprung into her arms.

29.

He kiss'd her lips, he kiss'd her burning cheek,
  Caress'd her young son in the fondest way,
A chain of gold was hung around her neck,   255
  And diamond bracelets shed the sparkling ray:
  Such kind and fond endearment did he pay,
The Abbot scarce from weeping could refrain.
  Nought good or bad could old Kincraigy say,
The farthest corner did his brow sustain,   260
And when they spoke to him he could not speak again.

30.

"Thou shalt be mine," the generous Minstrel said;
  "If I had known my love's unhappy state,
Not all the land my presence should have staid!
  Thou hast been injured, and my blame is great!   265
  This night the holy Abbot we'll entreat
To join our hands, then art thou doubly mine;
  Then hie thee back to Tay, for I must wait
Our Sovereign's will; but do not thou repine,
For all thy native hills, from Tay to Bran, are thine.   270

31.

"I have some favour with our Monarch's ear,
  And he hath kindly granted my request;
If this our son his royal name may bear,
  That his shall be an earldom of the best.
  I have his signet, and his high behest   275
To turn the ruthless Albert to the door:
  The royal bounds, that border to the west,
He grants thee too—these all are thine secure,
And every dame on Tay shall stoop to Ila Moore.

32.

"Haply to distant land I now may roam,   280
   But next when summer flowers the highland lea,
I will return, and seek my woodland home
   Within the bowers of sweet Kinnaird with thee.
   There is a lowly spot beneath the tree,
O'ershadow'd by the cliff—thou know'st it well!   285
   In that sweet solitude our cot shall be;
There first we loved, and there in love we'll dwell,
And long, long shall it stand, a Minstrel's faith to tell.

33.

"When summer eve hath wove her silken screen,
   Her fairy net-work of the night and day,   290
Hath tipt with flame the cone of mountain green,
   And dipt the red sun in the springs of Tay,
   How sweet with thee above the cliff to stray,
And see the evening stretch her starry zone!
   Or, shaded from the sun's meridian ray,   295
Lie stretch'd upon the lap of greenwood lone!
O happier shalt thou be for sorrows undergone!"

34.

Their hands were join'd—a mother's heart was blest!
   Her son was christen'd by his Sovereign's name;
In gold and scarlet the young imp was dress'd,   300
   A tiar on his head of curious frame.
   But ne'er on earth was seen a minstrel's dame
Shine in such beauty, and such rich array!
   An hundred squires, and fifty maidens, came
Riding on palfreys, sporting all the way,   305
To guard this splendid dame home to her native Tay.

35.

Needs not to sing of after joys that fell,
   Of years of glory and felicity;
Needs not on time and circumstance to dwell.—
   All who have heard of maid of low degree,   310
   Hight Ila Moore, up raised in dignity
And rank all other Scottish dames above,
   May well conceive who Mador needs must be,
And trace the winding mysteries of his love.
To such my tale is told, and such will it approve.   315

Conclusion

RETURN, my Harp, unto the Border dale,
  Thy native green hill, and thy fairy ring;
No more thy murmurs on the Grampian gale
  May wake the hind in covert slumbering,
  Nor must thy proud and far outstretched string   5
Presume to renovate the northern song,
  Wakening the echoes Ossian taught to sing;
Their sleep of ages still they must prolong,
Till son inspired is born their native hills among.

Loved was the voice that woo'd from Yarrow bowers   10
  Thy truant flight to that entrancing clime;
She ween'd thy melody and tuneful powers,
  Mellow'd by custom, and matured by time,
  Or that the sounds and energies sublime,
That darkly dwell by cataract and steep,   15
  Would rouse anew thy visionary chime,
Too long by southland breezes lull'd asleep.
O may she well approve thy wild and wandering sweep!

Should her fair hand bestow the earliest bays,
  Although proud learning lift the venom'd eye,   20
Still shalt thou warble strains of other days,
  Struck by some tuneful spirit lingering nigh;
  Till those, who long have pass'd derisive by,
Shall list to hear thy tones when newly strung,
  And Scottish maidens over thee shall sigh,   25
When I am all un-named by human tongue,
And thy enchanted chords by other hands are rung!

THE END

Appendix I
The Harper's Song

'The Harper's Song', which appears towards the end of Canto I of *Mador of the Moor*, is difficult to understand because it is written in Hogg's approximation of Middle Scots, the language of Lowland Scotland in the medieval period. However, it is argued in this edition's Introduction (pp. xxxvii–xxxviii) that 'The Harper's Song' is of great thematic importance. In 'The Harper's Song' an old man whose time has gone leaves Scotland after the arrival of a new and beautiful baby; and this calls forth a song of welcome and lament, sung by the unearthly inhabitants of fairyland. The old man can be identified with ancient Superstition; and the baby can be identified with the heavenly Grace of the new Christian religion that replaces Superstition.

Hogg lived in a Scotland deeply influenced by the ideas of the Scottish Enlightenment, that is to say in a world in which advanced thinkers tended to assume that the barbarity and superstition of uncivilised people were giving way before enlightenment, progress, and modern rationality. 'The Harper's Song', like *Mador of the Moor* as a whole, subverts this pattern by offering an alternative that is willing to be sceptical about the Scottish Enlightment's confident dismissal of pre-Enlightenment 'peasant' culture. Some of the ideas that underlie 'The Harper's Song' also find expression in Hogg's poem 'Superstition', published in his *Pilgrims of the Sun* (Edinburgh: Blackwood; London: Murray, 1815), pp. 129–48. In 'Superstition' Hogg deplores the 'cold saturnine morn' that has dawned on a post-Enlightenment Scotland, and celebrates the potentially life-enhancing and poetic power of ancient popular traditions of the supernatural. However, the 'mysterious dignity' of Superstition has been lost in the modern world, 'And true Devotion wanes away with her; | While in loose garb appears Corruption's harbinger' (*Pilgrims*, pp. 138, 131).

As is pointed out in the Introduction (p. xv), 'The Harper's Song' was removed from the text of *Mador* in *The Poetical Works of James Hogg*, 4 vols (Edinburgh: Constable; London: Hurst, Robinson, 1822), and also from subsequent reprints. However, it was reprinted as a separate poem in the 1822 *Poetical Works* as 'The Gyre Caryl' (II, 167–78). Hogg subsequently revised the poem, and made it more linguistically accessible, for publication in the annual *The Bijou* for 1829. This revised version was entitled 'Superstition and Grace', and it was subsequently included in Hogg's *A Queer Book* (Edinburgh: Blackwood; London: Cadell, 1832). In order to enhance its accessibility, and in order to facilitate comparison of Hogg's versions of this text, 'The Harper's Song' from the first edition of *Mador of the Moor* is printed below in parallel with the text of 'Superstition and Grace' in *A Queer Book*, ed. by P. D. Garside (S/SC, 1995), pp. 189–92: see also the editorial annotation at pp. 263–64. Writing of 'Superstition and Grace' Garside points out (p. 263): 'In subject matter and much of its wording the present poem derives directly from "The Gyre Caryl"'. He adds (p. 264) that collation 'shows how Hogg thinned out much of his original "ancient stile", transposed certain passages, and also removed some of the more arcane chants in the earlier poem'.

The Harper's Song

There wals ane auld caryl wonit in yon howe,
   Lemedon! lemedon! ayden lillelu!
His face was the geire, and his hayre was the woo,
   Sing Ho! Ro! Gillan of Allanhu!
But och! quhan the mure getis his cuerlet gray, &c.
Quhan the gloamyng hes flauchtit the nychte and the day, &c.
Quhan the crawis haif flowin to the greinwode schaw,
And the kydde hes blet owr the Lammer Law;
Quhan the dewe hes layde the klaiver asteep,
And the gowin hes fauldit hir buddis to sleep
Quhan nochte is herde but the merlinis mene—
Och! than that gyre caryl is neuir his lene!

   Ane bonnye baby, se meike and mylde,
Ay walkis wythe hym the dowie wylde:
The gowlin getis of sturt and stryffe,
And wearie wailis of mortyl lyffe,
Wald all be hushit till endlesse pece
At ane blynke of that babyis fece!

   Hir browe se fayre, and her ee se meike,
And the damyske roz that blumis on her cheike;
Hir lockis, and the bend of her bonnye bree,
And hir smyle mochte waukin the deide to see!

   Hir snoode, befryngit with mony a geme,
Wals stouin fra the raynbowe's brychtest beme;
And hir raile, mair quhyte than snawye dryfte,
Wals neuir wovin anethe the lyfte;
It keust sikn lychte on hill and gaire,
It shawit the wylde deer til hir laire;
And the fayries wakinit fra their beddis of dewe,
And they sang ane hyme, and the hyme was new!
List, lordyngs, list! for neuir agayne
Shalt' heire sikn wylde wanyirdlye strayne.
For they sang the nychte-gale in ane swoone,
And they sang the goud lockes fra the moone;
They sang the reidbreiste fra the wud,
And the laueroke out of the merlit clud;
And sum wee feres of bludeless byrthe
Cam out of the wurmholes of the yirthe,
And swoofit se lychtlye round the lee,
That they waldna kythe to mortyl ee;
But their erlisch sang it rase se shill,

Superstition and Grace
An Unearthly Ballad
By the Ettrick Shepherd

There was an auld carle won'd under yon shaw,
His cheek was the clay, and his hair was the snaw;
His brow was as glazed as a winter night,
But mingled with lines of immortal light;
And forth from his livid lips there flew
A flame of a lurid murky hue.
But there was a mystery him within
That roused up the twangs and terrors of sin;
And there was a gleide in that auld carle's ee,
That the saint and the sinner baith trembled to see.

But, oh! when the moor gat her coverlet gray,
When the gloaming had flaughted the night and the day,
When the craws had flown to the greenwood shaw,
And the kid blett over the Lammer law;
When the dew had laid the valley asteep,
And the gowan had fauldit her buds to sleep;
When naething was heard but the merlin's maen,
Oh then that gyre carle was never his lane.
A bonny wee baby sae meek and mild,
Then walked with him in the dowy wild;
But, oh! nae pen that ever grew
Could describe that baby's heavenly hue:
Yet all the barmings of sturt and strife,
And weary wailings of morteel life,
Would soon have been hushed to endless peace
At ae blink of that baby's face.

Her brow sae fair and her ee sae meek,
And the pale rose-bloom upon her cheek;
Her locks, and the bend of her sweet ee-bree,
And her smile might have wakened the dead to see.
Her snood befringed wi' many a gem
Was stown frae the rainbow's brightest hem;
And her rail, mair white than the snowy drift,
Was never woven aneath the lift;
It threw sic a light on the hill and the gair
That it showed the wild deer to her lair;
And the brown bird of the moorland fell
Upraised his head from the heather bell,
For he thought that his dawning of love and mirth,
Instead of the heaven was springing from earth;
And the fairies waken'd frae their beds of dew,

[*The Harper's Song*]

That the waesum tod youlit on the hill!
O lordyngs, list the cronach blande!
The flycherynge songe of Fayrie-land!

The Song of the Fairies.

SING AYDEN! AYDEN! LILLELU!
Bonnye bairne, we sing to you!
Up the Quhyte, and doune the Blak,
No ane leuer, no ane lak,
No ane shado at ouir bak;
No ane stokyng, no ane schue,
No ane bendit blever blue,
No ane traissel in the dewe!
Bonnye bairn, we sing to you,
AYDEN! AYDEN! LILLELU! &c.

    Speile! speile!
      The moone-rak speile!
Warre the rowar, warre the steile,
Throu the rok and throu the reile,
Rounde about lyke ane spynning wheile;
Throu the libbert, throu the le,
Rounde the yirde and rounde the se,
Bonnye bairne, we sing to thee,
Rounde the blumis and bellis of dewe,
AYDEN! AYDEN! LILLELU!

    Speide! speide!
      Lyving or deide!
Faster than the fyirie gleide,
Biz throu Laplin's tyrling dryfte!
Rounde the moone, and rounde the lyfte,
Aye we ring, and aye we sing
Our hune! hune!
And ante-tune!
Neuir! neuir! neuir dune!
Up the Leider and doune the Dye
Ay we sing our lullabye!
Bonnye bairne, we sing to you,
AYDEN! AYDEN! LILLELU!

    Ryng! ryng!
      Daunce and sing!

[Superstition and Grace]

And they sang a hymn, and that hymn was new.
Oh! Ladies list—for never again
Shalt thou hear sic a wild unearthly strain.
For they sang the night-breeze in a swoon,
And they sang the goud locks frae the moon:
They sang the redbreast frae the wood,
And the laverock out o' the marled cloud;
The capperkyle frae the bosky brae,
And the seraphs down frae the milky way;
And some wee feres of bloodless birth
Came out o' the worm-holes o' the earth,
And swoof'd sae lightly round the lea,
That they wadna kythe to mortal ee;
While the eldrich sang it rase sae shrill
That the waesome tod yooled on the hill:
Oh! Ladies list—for the choral band
Thus hymned the song of Fairy-land.

Song of the Fairies

Sing! sing! How shall we sing
Round the babe of the Spirits' King?
How shall we sing our last adieu,
Baby of life when we sing to you?
Now the little night-burdie may cheip i' the wa',
The plover may whew and the cock may craw;
For the bairny's sleep is sweet and sure,
And the maiden's rest is blest and pure,
Through all the links of the Lammer-muir:
Sin our bonny baby was sent frae heaven,
She comes o'ernight with the dew of even;
And when the day-sky buds frae the main,
She swaws wi' the dew to heaven again;
But the light shall dawn, and the howlet flee,
The dead shall quake, when the day shall be,
That she shall smile in the gladsome noon,
And sleep and sleep in the light of the moon.
Then shall our hallelues wake anew,
With harp and viol and ayril true.
      But well-a-day!
      How shall we say
Our earthly adieu ere we pass away?
How shall we hallow this last adieu,
Baby of life when we sing to you?
      Ring! ring!
      Dance and sing,

[The Harper's Song]

Hiche on the brume yer garlandis hyng!
For the bairnis sleipe is sweite and sure,
And the maydenis reste is blist and pure
Throu all the lynkis of Lammer-mure;
Sen our bonnye baby was sent fra heven.
Scho comis owrnycht withe the dewe of even,
And quhan the sone keikes out of the maine,
Scho swawis with the dewe to heven again.
But the lychte shall dawne and the houlat flee,
The deide shall ake, and the day shall be
Quhan scho shall smyle in the gladsum noone,
And sleipe and sleipe in the lychte of the moone!
Then shall our luias weke anewe,
With herpe and vele and ayril too,
To AYDEN! AYDEN! LILLELU!

Hyde! hyde!
Quhateuir betyde,
Elfe and dowle that ergh to byde!
The littil wee burdie mai cheipe in the wa,
The plevir mai sing, and the coke mai craw;
For neuir ane spyrit derke and doure
Dar raike the creukis of Lammer-mure;
And everilke gaiste of gysand hue
Shall melt in the breize our baby drew!
But we ar left in the grein-wud glen,
Bekaus we luf the chylder of men,
Sweitlye to sing our flawmand new;
Bonnye bairne, we sing to you,
AYDEN! AYDEN! LILLELU!

Pace! pace!
Spyritis of grace!
Sweite is the smyle of our babyis face!
The kelpye dernis, in dreide and dule,
Deipe in the howe of his eirye pule;
Gil-Moules frehynde the hallen mene fle,
Throu the dor-threshil, and throu the dor-ke,
And the mer-mayde mootes in the saifrone se.
But we ar left in the greine-wud glen,
Bekaus we luf the chylder of men,
Sweitlye to sing and neuir to rue,
Sweitlye to sing our last adue;
Bonnye bairne, we sing to you,
AYDEN! AYDEN! LILLELU!

[Superstition and Grace]

And on the green broom your garlands hing;
Hallow the hopes of this ray of grace,
For sweet is the smile of our baby's face;
And every ghaist of gysand hew
Has melted away in the breeze she drew;
The kelpie may dern in dread and dool,
Deep in the howe of his eiry pool;
Gil-moules frae hind the hallan may flee,
Through by the threshold, and through by the key,
And the mermaid moote in the safron sea:
But we are left in the greenwood glen,
Because we love the children of men,
Sweetly to sing, and never to rue,
Till now that we hymn our last adieu;
Baby of life we sing it to you!
    Sing! sing!
    How shall we sing
Round the babe of the Spirits' King?
Hither the breezes of elfland bring,
Then fairies away—away on the wing!
We now maun flit to a land of bliss,
To a land of holy silentness;
To a land where the night-wind never blew,
But thy fair spring shall ever be new;
When the moon shall wake nae mair to wane,
And the cloud and the rainbow baith are gane,
In bowers aboon the break o' the day,
We'll sing to our baby for ever and ay.

Then the carle beheld them swoof alang,
And heard the words of their fareweel sang.
They seem'd to ling asklent the wind,
And left a pathway of light behind;
But he heard them singing as they flew,
'Baby of life, adieu! adieu!
Baby of grace we sing to you!'

Then the carle he kneeled to that seraph young,
And named her with a tremulous tongue;
And the light of God shone on his face
As he looked to Heaven and named her GRACE;
And he barred the day of sorrow and pain
Ever to thrall the world again:
Then he clasped his hands and wept full sore,
When he bade her adieu for evermore.

[The Harper's Song]

  Sing! sing!
  How shall we sing
Rounde the bairne of the spiritis Kyng!
Lillelu! lillelu! mount in a ryng!
Fayries away! away on the wyng!
We too maune flytt to ane land of blisse!
To ane land of holy silentnesse!
To ane land quhair the nycht-wynd neuir blewe!
But thy fayre spryng shall euir be newe!
Quhan the moone shall waik ne mayre to wane,
And the clud and the raynbowe baithe are gane,
In bowirs aboone the brik of the day
We'll sing to our baby for ever and ay!

  Than the caryl he saw them swoof alang,
And he herde the wordis of thair leifu sang;
They seemit to lyng asklent the wynde,
And left ane streamourie trak behynde;
But he heirit them singyng as they flew,
AYDEN! AYDEN! LILLELU!

  Than the caryl liftit the babe se yung,
And nemit hir with ane tremilous tung;
And the lychte of God strak on his face
As he nelit on the dewe, and callit her Grace:
And he barrit the day of sorrowe and reuth
To flee fra the bairne of Hevenly Truthe;
And he barrit the deidis that nurice paine
Euir to thrall the worild again.
Than he claspit his handis, and wepit ful sair,
Quhan he bade hir adue for evirmaire.
O neuir wals babyis smyle se meike
Quhan scho fand the teir drap on her cheike!
And neuir wals babyis leuke se wae
Quhan scho saw the leil auld caryl gae!
But all his eiless ouphen trayne,
And all his gaistis and gyis war gane;
The gleides that gleimit in the derksome schaw,
And his fayries had flown the last of a':
Than the puir auld caryl was blythe to fle
Away fra the emerant isle of the se,
And neuir mayre seikis the walkis of men,
Unless in the diske of the glomyng glen.

[Superstition and Grace]

Oh! never was baby's smile so meek
When she felt the tear drop on her cheek;
And never was baby's look so wae
When she saw the stern auld carle gae;
But a' his eeless and elfin train,
And a' his ghaists and gyes were gane:
The gleids that gleamed in the darksome shaw,
And his fairies had flown the last of a'.
Then the poor auld carle was blithe to flee
Away frae the queen isle of the sea,
And never mair seeks the walks of men,
Unless in the disk of the gloaming glen.*

MOUNT BENGER
May 7th, 1828

---

* An edition of this ballad was published long ago by some other name. It is
now so entirely altered that only a few lines of the original remain.

J. H.

The Popular Context
Suzanne Gilbert

Hogg uses quotations from Scottish ballads and songs to introduce the cantos of *Mador of the Moor* and alludes to such traditional material frequently throughout the poem. In some cases, the relevance of an epigraph to the poem is very obvious, as with the Argument to Canto Third: 'Waly, Waly, Gin Love Be Bonny', a traditional song of love betrayed, might easily be imagined as Ila Moore's song following her abandonment by Mador. Ballad narratives used in other, very subtle ways further ground the literary poem in oral tradition and popular culture. This appendix signals some of the most significant strands contributing to the web of tradition underpinning the poem and provides information too detailed for the editorial Notes. The overall impression is that Hogg was comfortable with the variation and multiplicity inherent in oral traditions, which often contradict the values of print tradition, and was perfectly willing to introduce his own variations.

For the Argument for Canto First, 'The Hunting', Hogg uses the first two stanzas of 'The Hunting of the Cheviot', no. 162B in Francis James Child's five-volume collection *The English and Scottish Popular Ballads* (Boston, 1882–98). This ballad was popularly known as 'Chevy Chase', and the variant Hogg quotes with modernised spelling was included by Thomas Percy in *Reliques of Ancient English Poetry* (4th edn, London: John Nichols, 1794): Percy also has a variant from a much older manuscript first printed in 1719. 'The Hunting of the Cheviot' also appeared in numerous broadsides and chapbooks during Hogg's time. Child notes, however, that the ballad itself was 'an old and a popular song at the middle of the sixteenth century' (III, 303); *The Complaynte of Scotlande* (1549) identifies the 'Hunttis of Chevet' as being sung by shepherds and among 'the sangis of natural music of the antiquite' (fol. 42). Most significant for Hogg's purposes was the premise of an aristocratic hunt for pleasure, which for the traditional ballad served only as the starting point for a narrative culminating in a tragic contest between Percy and Douglas. In the stanzas excerpted for *Mador of the Moor*, the child 'that is unborn' who will 'rue [. . .] the hunting of that day' takes on a different meaning in the context of Hogg's poem.

The recurring motif of disguise and revelation is supported by Hogg's sometimes oblique allusions to another traditional ballad family, including 'The Jolly Beggar' (Child 279), which first appeared in David Herd's *Ancient and Modern Scottish Songs* (1776), and a similar ballad called 'The Gaberlunzie Man' (given by Child in an Appendix), which first appeared in Allan Ramsay's *The Tea-Table Miscellany* (1724). A common title in broadside form, the ballad also had a healthy life in oral tradition (see Emily Lyle, *Scottish Ballads* (Edinburgh: Canongate, 1994), p. 270). In this narrative, a beggar visits a farm and seduces the farmer's daughter; later he is revealed to be a rich gentleman. Percy prefaces 'The Gaberlunzie Man. A Scottish Song' with the following:

> Tradition informs us that the author of this song was K. JAMES V. of Scotland. This prince (whose character for wit and libertinism bears a great resemblance to that of his gay successor Charles II.) was noted for strolling about his dominions in disguise, and for his frequent gallantries with country girls. Two adventures of this kind he hath celebrated with his own pen, viz. in this ballad of THE GABERLUNZIE MAN; and in another intitled THE JOLLY BEGGAR ' [...] (4th edn, II, 60).

A footnote adds that his disguises were of 'a tinker, a begger, &c.', and 'Thus he used to visit a smith's daughter at Niddry, near Edinburgh'. Emily Lyle writes that the ballad's beggar-gentleman 'has been associated, though not in the wording of the ballad itself, with James V' (p. 270). Murray Pittock links 'James V's antics as a gaberlunzie' to 'the most popular of all Jacobite song groups, that of "The Bonnie Highland Laddie"', and adds, 'It is likely that the traditions attached to James V became merged with the virile imagery of the Highland / gipsy abduction song' (see Hogg, *Jacobite Relics: Second Series*, ed. by Murray G. H. Pittock (S/SC, 2003), pp. 509–10; and this edition's Introduction, pp. xxi–xxii).

For the Argument of Canto Second, 'The Minstrel', Hogg modifies lines from the broadside *The Taylor of Hogerglen's Wedding* (Edinburgh, 1776), which begins 'There came a taylor here to sew'. Robert Burns had moulded the song into 'The Taylor' for James Johnson's *The Scots Musical Museum*, but the chorus remained the same (*The Poems and Songs of Robert Burns*, ed. by James Kinsley, 3 vols (Oxford: Clarendon Press, 1968), II, 872):

> The Taylor he cam here to sew,
>   And weel he kend the way to woo,
> For ay he pree'd the lassie's mou
>   As he gaed but and ben O.
>
> Chorus
> For weel he kend the way O
>   The way O, the way O,
> For weel he kend the way O
>   The lassie's heart to win O. –

There are additional sources for the Argument of Canto Second. Though the subject-matter of the traditional ballad 'The Twa Sisters' (Child 10) differs completely, Hogg's incorporation of the phrase 'there cam a fiddler' verbally echoes lines from some variants of that ballad common in oral tradition at the time.

Another traditional song, 'Charlie is my Darling', also comes into play here. Hogg includes two versions in his collection of Jacobite songs (see Hogg, *Jacobite Relics: Second Series*, ed. by Murray G. H. Pittock (S/SC, 2003, pp. 92–94): a 'modern' one containing his own alterations, and an 'original' one based very closely on Burns's version (which Kinsley describes as a 'lyric reduction of a long romantic street ballad' from around 1775). Kinsley notes Burns's revisions of the traditional 'street ballad', particularly in changing the line 'For he had on his trousers' to 'For brawlie weel he ken'd the way'. Clearly, the song was well-known and widespread in oral tradition. In his edition of *Jacobite Relics* Murray Pittock quotes Wilkie's observation that 'There are a great many variations of this song often heard, among farm servants & cottagers' (p. 506). Central to the song is the motif of a royal seducing a commoner. Hogg's 'original' version reads (pp. 93–94):

> 'Twas on a Monday morning,
>   Right early in the year,
> That Charlie came to our town,
>   The young Chevalier.
>   And Charlie he's my darling,
>   My darling, my darling,
>   And Charlie he's my darling,
>   The young Chevalier.
>
> As he was walking up the street,
>   The city for to view,
> O there he spied a bonny lass,
>   The window looking through.
>   And Charlie he's my darling, &c.
>
> Sae light's he jumped up the stair,
>   And tirled at the pin;
> And wha sae ready as hersel
>   To let the laddie in!
>   And Charlie he's my darling, &c.
>
> He set his Jenny on his knee,
>   All in his Highland dress;
> *For brawly weel he kend the way*
>   *To please a bonny lass.* (emphasis added)
>   And Charlie he's my darling, &c.
>
> It's up yon heathery mountain,
>   And down yon scroggy glen,
> We daurna gang a-milking
>   For Charlie and his men.
>   And Charlie he's my darling, &c.

Conflating the two songs, 'The Taylor' and 'Charlie is My Darling', produces Hogg's Mador, fiddler-minstrel and royal in one, who seduces the country lass Ila Moore.

   The source of the Argument introducing Canto Fourth, 'The Palmer', is unidentified and may be Hogg's own creation. However, the 'puir auld man, | That doughtna live, and coudna die', a 'waesome sight' who 'spak to the spirits a' night lang', recalls the figure of the Wandering Jew, the Roman who according to legend taunted Jesus on his way to the crucifixion, and thus was condemned to guilt-stricken immortality, and to repeating his story forever. This figure was hugely popular in Romantic literature (for example, it lies behind Coleridge's 'The Rime of the Ancient Mariner' and Matthew Gregory Lewis's *The Monk*), thanks in part to Percy's inclusion of the ballad 'The Wandering Jew' in the *Reliques* (4th edn, II, 301–07):

> No resting could he finde at all,
> No ease, nor hearts content;
> No house, nor home, nor biding place:
> But wandring forth he went
> From towne to towne in foreigne landes,
> With grieved conscience still,
> Repenting for the heinous guilt
> Of his fore-passed ill. (ll. 49–56)

Hogg's introduction of the Palmer suggests another important strand from tradition. As is pointed out in this edition's Notes, the Palmer's life-story (as he tells it to Ila in Canto IV of *Mador of the Moor*) echoes the situation and events of the traditional ballad 'The Cruel Mother' (Child 20). The same basic situation is also echoed in Ila's own life-story, but the heroine of Hogg's poem responds to her plight in a much more positive way than does the cruel mother of the ballad. A variant of 'The Cruel Mother' appears (under the title 'Lady Anne') in the third volume of Walter Scott's *Minstrelsy of the Scottish Border* (1803). Hogg would certainly have known this ballad from the *Minstrelsy*, and he would also have known variants of it from the oral tradition of his native Ettrick, as well as from other print sources such as David Herd's *Ancient and Modern Scottish Songs* (1776). Mention should be made of 'The Maid and the Palmer' (Child 21), also known as 'The Maid of Coldingham', based on the biblical story of the meeting of Christ and the Woman of Samaria in John 4 (see David Buchan, 'The Maid, the Palmer, and the Cruel Mother', *Malahat Review*, 3 (1967), pp. 98–99). This ballad connects interestingly with 'The Cruel Mother', and with Canto IV of *Mador of the Moor*. The stern palmer (or the 'eldern man') of the traditional ballad reveals the crime committed by the 'cruel mother' at the well and pronounces a terrible sentence on her. The Palmer of Hogg's poem, on the other hand, has himself made grievous human errors which in fact contributed to a maiden's downfall, and to her committing infanticide (thereby becoming a 'cruel mother'); he understands Ila Moore's situation and, as part of atoning for his own sins, serves as protector to both mother and child. As characters, neither Ila Moore nor the Palmer fit neatly into the ballad paradigm, and in Hogg's development of the ballad tradition both are candidates for grace and redemption.

In his introductory note to 'Lady Anne' in the *Minstrelsy*, Scott quotes a 'fragment' of the ballad 'which I have often heard sung in my childhood'. This 'fragment' finds its place in Child as 20Bb, but Child relegates Scott's main text to an Appendix, explaining in a footnote: ' "Lady Anne," in Scott's

Minstrelsy, III, 259, 1803, is on the face of it a modern composition, with extensive variations, on the theme of the popular ballad'. As the ballad known as 'The Cruel Mother' or 'Lady Anne' is of clear thematic importance for *Mador of the Moor*, it may be useful to quote Scott's introductory note:

THIS ballad was communicated to me by Mr Kirkpatrick Sharpe of Hoddom, who mentions having copied it from an old magazine. Although it has probably received some modern corrections, the general turn seems to be ancient, and corresponds with that of a fragment, containing the following verses, which I have often heard sung in my childhood:

> She set her back against a thorn,
> And there she has her young son borne;
> "O smile nae sae, my bonny babe!
> An ye smile sae sweet, ye'll smile me dead."

> *   *   *   *   *

> An' when that lady went to the church,
> She spied a naked boy in the porch.

> "O bonny boy, an' ye were mine,
> I'd cleed ye in the silks sae fine."
> "O mither dear, when I was thine,
> To me ye were na half sae kind."

> *   *   *   *   *

Stories of this nature are very common in the annals of popular superstition. It is, for example, currently believed in Ettrick Forest, that a libertine, who had destroyed fifty-six inhabited houses, in order to throw the possessions of the cottagers into his estate, and who added, to this injury, that of seducing their daughters, was wont to commit, to a carrier in the neighbourhood, the care of his illegitimate children, shortly after they were born. His emissary regularly carried them away, but they were never again heard of. The unjust and cruel gains of the profligate laird were dissipated by his extravagance, and the ruins of his house seem to bear witness to the truth of the rhythmical prophecies denounced against it, and still current among the peasantry. He himself died an untimely death; but the agent of his amours and crimes survived to extreme old age. When on his death-bed, he seemed much oppressed in mind, and sent for a clergyman, to speak peace to his departing spirit. But, before the messenger returned, the man was in his last agony; and the terrified assistants had fled from his cottage, unanimously averring, that the wailing of the murdered infants had ascended from behind his couch, and mingled with the groans of the departing sinner.

Scott's main text of the ballad is as follows:

Lady Anne

FAIR lady Anne sate in her bower,
    Down by the greenwood side,
And the flowers did spring, and the birds did sing,
    'Twas the pleasant May-day tide.

But fair lady Anne on sir William call'd,
    With the tear grit in her e'e,
"O though thou be fause, may heaven thee guard,
    In the wars ayont the sea!"

Out of the wood came three bonnie boys,
    Upon the simmer's morn,
And they did sing, and play at the ba',
    As naked as they were born.

"O seven lang year wad I sit here,
    Amang the frost and snaw,
A' to hae but ane o' these bonnie boys,
    A playing at the ba'."—

Then up and spake the eldest boy,
    "Now listen, thou fair ladie!
And ponder well the read that I tell,
    Then make ye a choice of the three.

"'Tis I am Peter, and this is Paul,
    And that ane, sae fair to see,
But a twelve-month sinsyne to paradise came,
    To join with our companie."

"O I will hae the snaw-white boy,
    The bonniest of the three."
"And if I were thine, and in thy propine*,
    O what wad ye do to me?"

"'Tis I wad clead thee in silk and gowd,
    And nourice thee on my knee."
"O mither! mither! when I was thine,
    Sic kindness I could na see."

"Beneath the turf, where now I stand,
    The fause nurse buried me;
The cruel penknife sticks still in my heart,
    And I come not back to thee."

*   *   *   *   *

* *Propine*—Usually gift, but here the power of giving or bestowing. [Scott's note.]

For the Argument of Canto Fifth, 'The Christening', Hogg quotes from the traditional ballad 'Child Maurice' (Child 83), variants of which were common in the eighteenth and nineteenth centuries. The stanzas he uses are similar to a variant recorded from oral tradition by his contemporary William Motherwell (83E), and nearly identical to stanzas in 'Gil Morrice. A Scottish Ballad' in Percy's *Reliques* (4th edn, III, 90–99; see on p. 97):

> I got ze in my father's house,
> Wi' mickle sin and shame;
> I brocht thee up in gude grene wode,
> Under the heavy rain.
> Oft have I by thy cradle sitten,
> And foldly seen thee sleip;
> But now I gae about thy grave,
> The saut tears for to weip.

Percy notes, 'Since it was first printed, the Editor has been assured that the foregoing Ballad is still current in many parts of Scotland' (p. 99). In the traditional ballad, the child is mistakenly murdered by his own father, and the stanza beginning with the mother sitting by the child's cradle concludes with the parallel, tragic image of her attending the child's grave. Hogg deletes the second half, thereby undercutting the tragic narrative: his poem will provide a positive outcome for Ila Moore and her child.

More broadly, for this canto Hogg draws on a family of ballads that involve the seduction and subsequent abandonment of the woman, a birth in the greenwood, and the eventual restoration of identity to (sometimes) the mother and (usually) the child, though sometimes in tragic circumstances. The last part of 'Gil Brenton' (Child 5), in which the woman's possession of a ring given by her lover reveals the truth of the child's parentage, fits the narrative of *Mador of the Moor* strikingly well. In ballads, the ring as 'keepsake, identification, and token of fidelity' is a significant motif (see Natascha Wurzbach and Simone M. Salz, *Motif Index of the English & Scottish Popular Ballads* (Berlin: Walter de Gruyter, 1995), p. 72). Variants of the formulaic construction in the Argument's second part, 'Gae rowe my young son in the silk, | An' lay my lady as white as the milk', may be found in several ballads, among them 'Gil Brenton' and the variant called 'Cospatrick' in Scott's *Minstrelsy*, 'Willie o Douglas Dale' (Child 101A), and 'Child Waters' (Child 63). For example, Child 63B has at stanza 35:

> Up he has taen his bonny young son,
>   An gard wash him wi the milk;
> An up has he taen his fair lady,
>   Gard row her in the silk.

As in the Greek story of Eros and Psyche, in 'Gil Brenton', 'Child Waters', and *Mador of the Moor* a woman is seduced and made pregnant, and then has to undergo a series of trials before her value is recognised and her rightful place asserted.

It appears from all this that *Mador of the Moor* has strong and deep roots in the traditional oral ballads familiar to Hogg from his Ettrick childhood. In this context it is interesting to note that work began on *Mador* in the autumn of 1813, only a few months after the publication of the first (1813) version of Hogg's most famous poem, *The Queen's Wake*. In his S/SC edition of *The Queen's Wake* (2004), Douglas Mack has argued that Hogg constructs the 1813 version of the *Wake* as a contest 'between rival aristocratic and popular strands within the Scottish poetic tradition', the aristocratic strand being associated with Macpherson's *Ossian* and with Scott's narrative poems, while the popular strand is associated with the old oral ballads and with Hogg's own poetry. It may be that in *Mador of the Moor* Hogg continues this contest between what he called Scott's poetic 'school o' chivalry' and his own ballad-based 'mountain an' fairy school'. (See *The Queen's Wake*, ed. by Douglas S. Mack (S/SC, 2004), pp. xxxiv–xxxv.)

Note on the Text

As this edition's Introduction points out, four printings of *Mador of the Moor* appeared in Hogg's lifetime. In Britain, the first edition of 1816 was published jointly by William Blackwood in Edinburgh and John Murray in London. This was followed by *Mador*'s appearance in the four-volume edition of Hogg's *Poetical Works* published in 1822 by Archibald Constable of Edinburgh in partnership with the London firm of Hurst, Robinson & Co. Across the Atlantic, *Mador* was published in Philadelphia in 1816 when Moses Thomas reprinted the first edition, and the poem also appeared in 1825 in D. Mallory's two-volume New York edition of Hogg's *Poetical Works*. To the best of this editor's knowledge, no manuscript version of the poem survives, nor do proofs.

A collation of the four printings that appeared during Hogg's lifetime reveals examples of the usual changes in 'accidentals' (that is to say, in punctuation, spelling, capitalisation, and the like) that were normally introduced in the early nineteenth century when texts were reprinted. One interesting feature of the American printings is that 'King' and 'Monarch', which are regularly capitalized in both Edinburgh printings, become lower-case 'king' and 'monarch'. In its own quiet way this indication of American attitudes to British royalty serves as a reminder that the conflict known as the War of 1812 in the United States, when the British army sacked and burned Washington D.C. including the White House, would have been fresh in the memories of the first American readers of *Mador of the Moor*. Hogg does not appear to have had any involvement in the preparation of either of the American printings, and their departures in wording from the text of the first edition are few and insignificant.

There is a substantial alteration in one of the early printings, however. In the Edinburgh 1822 *Poetical Works* 'The Harper's Song' in Canto I, which is structurally and thematically significant, was removed from *Mador of the Moor* and was printed as a separate poem entitled 'The Gyre Caryl' (see the present edition's Appendix I for further details). Some small changes in wording are also introduced in *Mador* in the 1822 *Poetical Works*, in order to allow the text to run smoothly in spite of this excision. In the first edition, Canto I stanza 31 introduces 'The Harper's Song' as follows: 'Bent was the minstrel's eye, and wild to see, | As thus he pour'd the visionary strain'. In 1822 'As thus' becomes 'The whilst', and the reader is therefore no longer led to expect that the minstrel's song will follow. Unlike the rest of *Mador of the Moor,* 'The Harper's Song' is not in Spenserian stanzas, and the first edition resumes the sequence of numbered stanzas immediately after the Song with stanza 32, which opens: 'The harper ceased'. In 1822 this becomes: 'And when he ceased'. In the first edition, the fourth line of this stanza refers to 'the old reverend sire' of whom the harper has just been singing, but in 1822 this phrase becomes 'some old reverend sire'. Likewise, in stanza 33 the first edition mentions 'the old carl of whom the minstrel sung', while 1822 has 'the unearthly strain the minstrel sung'. Both

American printings include 'The Harper's Song', and follow the first edition's readings in stanzas 31–33. However, the 1822 text, with 'The Harper's Song' removed, became the standard version of Hogg's poem, as it was reprinted in the various Victorian posthumous collected editions of his works, including the Blackie edition of 1865 reproduced in the widely-used AMS reprint of 1973. As a result of the omission of 'The Harper's Song', Hogg's major themes and concerns in *Mador* have been short-circuited and thwarted: as is shown in the Introduction above, the poem is not only modified, but seriously weakened because of this omission. Why, then, was the omission originally made in the 1822 *Poetical Works*, and by whom was it made?

The surviving documentary evidence does not supply a clear answer to these questions. However, it is possble to make some deductions. Various changes of direction had recently taken place in Hogg's life around the time, late in 1821, when he engaged in negotiations about a projected edition of his *Poetical Works*, the edition which was duly published by Constable in four volumes in June 1822. In the spring of 1821, recently married and in his early fifties, Hogg had taken on a nine-year lease of a large farm (Mount Benger) in Yarrow. Complications were soon to follow, however. As Norah Parr records, his well-to-do father-in-law Peter Phillips had offered financial help with regard to the stocking of the new farm, but shortly after Hogg had signed the lease for Mount Benger his father-in-law suffered a severe and unexpected financial loss, which meant that the promised help could no longer be forthcoming (see Norah Parr, *James Hogg at Home* (Dollar: Douglas Mack, 1980), p. 18). Then in June 1821 Hogg's publishers Oliver and Boyd unexpectedly turned down his new novel *The Three Perils of Man*. A further blow came in August, when a savage review in *Blackwood's Edinburgh Magazine* of his 'Memoir of the Life of James Hogg' prompted Hogg to leave the *Blackwood's* camp (where he had become well established), and to begin writing for the time being for Constable's less successful rival the *Edinburgh Magazine*. After these various setbacks, and urgently needing money to stock his new farm, Hogg in the early months of 1822 badly needed to come to a speedy and favourable arrangement with Constable with regard to the projected *Poetical Works*.

In these circumstances, Hogg seems to have taken a real interest in the preparation of the 1822 *Poetical Works*, without undertaking a serious and sustained revision of every text in the collection. For example, in a letter of 8 February 1822 he urges Constable to 'be sure to take the *fifth* or *sixth edition*' of *The Queen's Wake* 'for the sake of the late additions'. In 1822 the fifth edition (1819) of Hogg's most famous poem is indeed reprinted, but without any sign of authorial re-engagement with the text (see Douglas Mack's S/SC edition of *The Queen's Wake* (2004), pp. lxxv, lxxxvi). Likewise, with the possible exception of the omission of 'The Harper's Song' and the consequent changes discussed above, there is no sign of authorial re-engagement with the text in the 1822 version of *Mador*. Verbal departures from the first edition text of this poem are few and insignificant in the 1822 *Poetical Works*. Canto I stanza 11 of the first edition offers a typical example of the few verbal changes that do exist. This stanza records that a herd of deer 'have found' a retreat, while in 1822 this becomes 'has found'. As with the non-verbal variation already discussed, early-nineteenth-century printers frequently introduced minor verbal changes when reprinting a text. Indeed, the printers of the 1822 *Poetical Works* may even have been responsible for the small verbal changes (discussed above) which are designed to make adjustments as a result of the removal of 'The Harper's Song'. These changes, while competently done, are minimal, and do not necessarily indicate authorial re-engagement with the text.

Some of the reviews of the first edition of *Mador* had expressed worries about 'The Harper's Song': for example, as the present edition's Introduction indicates (p. xviii), the *Critical Review* had complained that the 'long harper's song [...] must be totally unintelligible to all who are not master of the rudest dialects of Scotland'. Clearly, then, there may well have been a feeling in 1822 that *Mador* would become more attractive to the reading public if 'The Harper's Song' were to be removed, and this no doubt explains why it is excised and reprinted as a separate poem in 1822. It may be that Hogg made this change of his own volition, or it may be that he acquiesced in this arrangement under pressure from his publishers. Either way, there seems to be no convincing artistic reason for the change: the 1822 version of the poem loses some of the complexity and resonance of Hogg's original first edition text. Commercial pressure seems a much more likely explanation. The S/SC edition therefore adopts the first edition as its copy-text, a decision that allows Hogg's poem to speak once again with its original force and vigour.

The S/SC edition of *Mador of the Moor* contains very few emendations of the 1816 copy-text. Some of the lines in stanza 8 of Canto II are wrongly indented in the first edition, and this has been corrected. The S/SC edition's other emendations are listed below. The relevant page number and line number is provided for each item, followed by first the emended text and then the reading of the first edition. In each case the emended reading adopts a change that had previously been made in the 1822 *Poetical Works*.

16, l. 41 on their mountain bed,] on their mountain bed
35, l. 82 sore his face,] sore his face
35, l. 83 with his eye,] with his eye
52, l. 38 sow!] sow
52, l. 46 thy vague unbodied lay!] thy vague unbodied lay
77, l. 65 heard her weep.] heard her weep
83, l. 293 stray,] stay,

Notes

In the Notes that follow, references to the text of *Mador of the Moor* include page and line numbers. Where it seems useful to discuss the meaning of particular phrases, this is done in the Notes: single words are dealt with in the Glossary. Quotations from the Bible are from the King James version, the translation most familiar to Hogg and his contemporaries. For references to plays by Shakespeare, the edition used has been *The Complete Works: Compact Edition*, ed. by Stanley Wells and Gary Taylor (Oxford: Clarendon Press, 1988). Quotations from letters by Hogg are from the first volume of the Stirling / South Carolina edition of Hogg's *Letters* (ed. by Gillian Hughes, 2004): in this edition Hogg's letters are arranged chronologically, and can be located by their date. For references to other volumes of the Stirling / South Carolina Edition the editor's name is given after the title, with the abbreviation 'S/SC' and date of first publication following in parentheses. In the Notes below, the National Library of Scotland is abbreviated as NLS and the title of the periodical *Studies in Hogg and his World* is abbreviated as *SHW*. The Notes are greatly indebted to standard works such as *The Oxford Dictionary of National Biography* (cited as *ODNB*), *The Oxford English Dictionary* (cited as *OED*), *The Oxford Dictionary of English Proverbs*, 3rd ed. (cited as *ODEP*), *The Edinburgh Edition of the Waverley Novels* (cited as *EEWN*), and *The Scottish National Dictionary* (cited as *SND*). References to 'Child' are to the ballad numbers in *The English and Scottish Popular Ballads*, ed. by Francis James Child, 5 vols (Boston: Houghton Mifflin, 1882–98). References to 'Kinsley' are to the poem numbers in *The Poems and Songs of Robert Burns*, ed. by James Kinsley, 3 vols (Oxford: Clarendon Press, 1968). Preparation of the Notes below has been greatly assisted by consultation of R. A. Houston and W. W. J. Knox, *The New Penguin History of Scotland* (London: Allen Lane, 2001); Michael Lynch, *Scotland: A New History* (London: Pimlico, 1992); and *The Oxford Companion to Scottish History*, ed. by Michael Lynch (Oxford: Oxford University Press, 2001). Texts frequently quoted in the Editorial Notes are referred to by the following abbreviations:

Groome: *Ordnance Gazetteer of Scotland: A Survey of Scottish Topography*, ed. by Francis H. Groome, 6 vols (Edinburgh: Jack, 1882–85). (Quotations from Groome in the Notes below are from the entries for the various places under discussion.)

Holinshed: Raphael Holinshed, *The Scottish Chronicle; or, A Complete History and Description of Scotland*, 2 vols (Arbroath: J. Findlay, 1805). (Hogg seems to have used this edition of a work first published in 1577: see the first of Hogg's Notes in his poem *The Queen's Wake*.)

'Memoir': Hogg's autobiographical 'Memoir of the Author's Life' and its continuation 'Reminiscences of Former Days' are quoted from his *Altrive Tales*, ed. by Gillian Hughes (S/SC, 2003).

The Silver Bough: F. Marian McNeill, *The Silver Bough: A Four Volume Study of the National and Local Festivals of Scotland*, 4 vols (Glasgow: MacLellan, 1957–68).

1 **Wild mirth of the desart! fit pastime for Kings! | Which still the rude Bard in his solitude sings** the quotation on the first edition's titlepage is from 'Address to a Wild Deer in the Forest of Dalness, Glen-Etive', by John Wilson (1785–1854), the 'Christopher North' of *Blackwood's Edinburgh Magazine*. This poem was included in Wilson's *The City of the Plague, and Other Poems* (Edinburgh: Constable, 1816). Writing about *Mador of the Moor* on 11 April 1816 to his publisher William Blackwood, Hogg comments 'I must have a motto the title page will be quite naked without it', and goes on to suggest either this quotation from Wilson, or (from *Hamlet*, I. 3. 45–46) 'I shall the effect of this good lesson keep | As watchman to my heart'.

3 **To Mr John Grieve** a minor Scottish poet, Grieve (1781–1836) found his primary employment as a prosperous Edinburgh hatter. His friendship with Hogg went back to their early years in Ettrick, and he gave Hogg much-needed financial support when Hogg moved to Edinburgh in 1810 to attempt to establish himself as a professional writer. Grieve was in partnership with Chalmers Izett, whose wife encouraged Hogg to write *Mador of the Moor* while the poet was visiting Kinnaird House, the home of the Izetts. Grieve, in addition to helping a number of struggling authors, contributed to various periodicals, and his work is included in Hogg's song-collection *The Forest Minstrel* (1810). The Fourteenth Bard, one of the competing minstrels in Hogg's *Queen's Wake* (1813), is a portrait of Grieve. For further information see Janette Currie's essay on 'James Hogg's Literary Friendships with John Grieve and Eliza Izett', which follows this edition's Introduction. See also 'Memoir', pp. 27, 48, 221, 228; Richard D. Jackson, '*The Pirate* and "The Bonny Lass of Deloraine"', *Scott Newsletter*, 40 (Summer 2002), 9–21, (pp. 15–19); Hogg, *The Queen's Wake*, ed. by Douglas S. Mack (S/SC, 2004), pp. xiv, xxv; and *The Collected Letters of James Hogg: Volume 1 1800–1819*, ed. by Gillian Hughes (S/SC, 2004), pp. 45, 457–60.

5 **Advertisement** refers to the marriage of Robert II, King of Scots (reigned 1371–1390) to Elizabeth Moore or Mure (see Introduction, p. xxi). Hogg uses the historical fact of this marriage as the jumping-off point for his fictional story in *Mador of the Moor*, and he uses Holinshed's account (II, 29–30) as his source. In Holinshed's version, Robert II

> had to wife at the time of his attaining the crown, *Eufemie*, daughter to *Hugh*, earl of *Ross*, by whom he had two sons, *Walter* and *David*. But before he was married to her he kept one *Elizabeth Mure*, in place of his wife, and had by her three sons, *John*, *Robert*, and *Alexander*, with divers daughters, of the which one was married to *John Dunbar*, earl of *Murrey*, and another to *John Leon*, lord of *Glames*. [...] His wife queen *Eufemie* deceased the third year after her husband attained the crowne, and then incontinentlie he married *Elizabeth Mure* (or *Moore*, daughter to Sir *Adam Mure*, knight,) his old lemman, to the end the children which he had by her might be made legitimate by vertue of the matrimonie subsequent. (Although before he had procured this *Elizabeth* to be given in matrimony to one *Gifford*, a nobleman in

Louthian, which also died (as fortune served) when *Eufemie*, first wife
of the said *Robert* died, whereby they (being now both at libertie)
might renew their own old love, and in wedlock possess that which
they had injoyed in adulterie.)

Holinshed's account here is broadly correct, but is not wholly reliable in
all its aspects. For fuller and more accurate accounts of Robert II's mar-
riage to Elizabeth Moore see the *ODNB* under Robert II, and Stephen
Boardman, *The Early Stewart Kings: Robert II and Robert III 1371–1406* (East
Linton: Tuckwell Press, 1996). In the event, John (eldest son of Robert II
and Elizabeth Mure or Moore) inherited the Scottish throne on his father's
death, taking the name Robert III. Robert II was the first Stuart king (see
note on 19, l. 168), and Elizabeth Moore's great-great-great-great-great-
great-grandson inherited the throne of England in 1603, in the person of
James VI of Scotland (James I of England). In *Mador of the Moor*, 'Elizabeth'
Moore becomes 'Isla' Moore—'on account of the rythm', as the Advertise-
ment puts it.

Introduction

9, ll. 1–9 Thou Queen of Caledonia's mountain floods [...] sons of men
Caledonia is a poetic reference to Scotland. The Tay is here being hailed as
the Queen of Scotland's mountain rivers, and Burns was one of the 'gifted
bards' who have sung its praises: see 'Written in the Inn at Kenmore'
(Kinsley 169). This opening stanza gives an apt overview of the landscape
through which the Tay runs from its source in the wild Highland landscape
of the Grampian Mountains of north central Scotland, to the fertile Low-
land scenery around its lower course and estuary. Groome writes (under
'Tay, The':

> a river draining the greater part of Perthshire and passing off to the
> sea between Forfarshire and Fifeshire. It issues from Loch Tay, or
> rather begins there to take the name of Tay; but it is really formed
> by two great head-streams which rise among the Grampians on the
> mutual border of Perth and Argyll shires. The northern stream bears
> successively the names of the BA, the GAUIR, and the TUMMEL;
> and, in its progress, it forms, by expansion of its waters, the three
> great lakes of LYDOCH or Laidon, RANNOCH, and TUMMEL. [...]
> The southern one of the great head-streams bears successively the
> names of the FILLAN, the DOCHART, and the Tay; and traverses, in
> its progress, Loch Dochart and Loch Tay. [...] The extent of surface
> drained by the Tay and its tributaries is computed at 2400 square
> miles.

9, l. 27 battlements of ancient liberty the Grampians are also seen as the
citadel of Scotland's ancient liberty in the opening lines of Hogg's epic
poem *Queen Hynde* (1824): see Hogg, *Queen Hynde*, ed. by Suzanne Gilbert
and Douglas S. Mack (S/SC, 1998), p. 5. Scotland's pride in its 'ancient
liberty' was based on the fact that the Highlands had remained uncon-
quered by the Romans, although the rest of the island of Great Britain
had fallen under Roman control.

10, l. 33 reddening moors when the moorland heather comes into bloom in
late summer.

10, l. 41 beetling cliffs o'erhang the belted plain aptly describes the landscape through which the Tay flows immediately downstream from Perth, as it completes the transition from the Highlands to the Lowlands. Here high cliffs overlook a fertile plain marked with the patterns of cultivation.

10. ll. 47–49 fertile vallies [...] the ocean's majesty these lines provide an apt description of the landscape through which the Tay flows between Perth and Dundee, as it opens out into the Firth of Tay before joining the North Sea.

10, l. 51 traffic bustles the busy city and seaport of Dundee is situated on the north bank of the Firth of Tay, as the river opens out to join the sea.

10, l. 56 Queen of green Albyn's rivers the specific reference is to the River Tay, but the allusion to Albyn conjures up ancient memories of Gaelic Scotland. Alba is the Gaelic name for the combined kingdom of the Picts and the Scots of Dalriada. '"Alba" or "Albaine" as it is called in *The Scottish Chronicle* evolved into the modern Scotland, and "Alba" remains the name for "Scotland" in modern Gaelic'. For further details see Hogg's *Queen Hynde,* ed. by Suzanne Gilbert and Douglas S. Mack (S/SC, 1998), p. 247.

10, l. 60 The wayward Minstrel of a southern dale as he emphasises in his self-portrait as the Bard of Ettrick in *The Queen's Wake* (1813), Hogg sees himself as a poet of the Borders in the south of Scotland, rather than a bard in the Highland tradition.

10, l. 63 To friendship, and to thee the poem is inspired, not only by the scenery of the Tay, but also by Hogg's friendship with Mrs Izett: see Introduction, p. xi.

11, ll. 64–72 Old Caledonia! [...] songs of magic charm this stanza is an allusion to Scott's famous lines which begin the second stanza of Canto V of *The Lay of the Last Minstrel* (1805):

> O Caledonia! stern and wild,
> Meet nurse for a poetic child!
> Land of brown heath and shaggy wood,
> Land of the mountain and the flood,
> Land of my sires! what mortal hand
> Can e'er untie the filial band,
> That knits me to thy rugged strand!

11, l. 70 southern pride and luxury in this phrase Hogg refers to the long enmity between the northern kingdom of Scotland and the southern realm of England. Sir Walter Scott in *Tales of a Grandfather* (1828) explains this enmity in historical terms, recounting the frequent battles between the Picts and the Scots of the north and the Britons of the south, noting the conquering of the south, first by Romans and then the Angles and Saxons. Scott emphasizes the hardiness of the Scots and the more indulgent nature of the Britons: see Walter Scott, *Tales of a Grandfather*, 3 vols (Edinburgh: Cadell, 1828), I, 7–18.

11, l. 81 Mountain Bard Hogg had first established his reputation as a poet with *The Mountain Bard* (Edinburgh: Constable; London: Murray, 1807).

11, l. 82 I cannot sing of Longcarty and Hay Luncarty (*Loncart* in Holinshed) lies about four miles to the north of Perth, near the Tay. According to Holinshed (I, 305–08), it was the site of a battle in 990 in which the invading Danes were about to overpower the Scottish forces of Kenneth

III when Hay (a ploughman) and his sons threw themselves into the battle, and succeeded in encouraging the Scots army and routing the Danes. Hay was rewarded with extensive land in Perthshire.

11, l. 84 Dunsinnan towers, or Birnam gray Dunsinane hill overlooks the Tay about eight miles north of Perth, and has vestiges of an ancient fort known as 'Macbeth's Castle'. There is an allusion here to the prophecy in Shakespeare's *Macbeth* that 'Macbeth shall never vanquished be until | Great Birnam Wood to high Dunsinane Hill | Shall come against him' (IV. 1. 108–10). In writing *Macbeth* Shakespeare drew on Holinshed's account of the reigns of Duncan and Macbeth (see I, 339–51 in the Arbroath edition used by Hogg).

11, l. 85 Where Canmore battled and the Villain fell the allusion is to Shakespeare's *Macbeth*, which ends with the triumph of Malcolm III (called Canmore), and the death of Macbeth.

11, l. 95 auburn locks it was usual to describe Highlanders as red-haired. For example, Rob Roy ('Red Robert') Macgregor was so called because of his profusion of red hair.

12, l. 100 Nature's simple Bard Hogg consistently presents himself as a self-taught poet, inspired by nature rather than art, and he often associates his poetry with the natural (as opposed to artificial) poetry of the Eolian harp. See, for example, the concluding lines of *The Queen's Wake* (1813); see also *Queen Hynde*, ed. Gilbert and Mack (S/SC, 1998), p. xl.

12, l. 105 his wild-wood lay an echo of Milton, 'L' Allegro': 'Then to the well-trod stage anon, | If Jonson's learned sock be on, | Or sweetest Shakespeare fancy's child | Warble his native wood-notes wild' (ll. 131–34). This passage from Milton is also echoed in the description of the Eighth Bard (who sings 'The Witch of Fife') in Hogg's *The Queen's Wake* (1813). A 'wild-wood lay' suggests a poet who is to be associated with the inspired natural spontaneity of Shakespeare, as opposed to the more ponderous learning of Ben Jonson.

Canto First: The Hunting

13 Argument Hogg quotes from the traditional ballad 'The Hunting of the Cheviot' (Child 162B). 'Chevy Chase' is the location of a battle between the English Percys and the Scottish Douglases, while 'Earl Percy' is Sir Henry Percy (1364–1403), known as Hotspur in Shakespeare's history plays. See also Appendix II at p. 96.

15, l. 1 Athol mountains Atholl or Athole is a mountainous district in the northern part of Perthshire, bounded to the north by the wild and spectacular Cairngorm Mountains in the Central Grampians. The rivers of Atholl are all, directly or indirectly, tributaries of the Tay, which lies a little to the south. 'Athole Forest is a part of the district preserved for deer and other game; comprises upwards of 100,000 acres; is famed above every other forest for its hunting attractions and its magnificent scenery; possessed, in former times, great immunities and privileges; belongs now to the Duke of Athole; is stocked with about 7000 red deer, and with numerous roe-deer; abounds with red and black game, plovers, partridges, and ptarmigans; has also multitudes of foxes, wild-cats, polecats, martins, weasels, and alpine hares; is frequented, in some parts, by the jay, the woodpecker, the kestrel, and the eagle; and possesses a rich variety of rare indigenous plants' (Groome).

15, l. 5 the rout of Scotland's gallant king *Mador of the Moor* follows Scott's *The Lady of the Lake* in devoting its first Canto to an account of a royal hunt in the Highlands. *OED* defines *rout* (9) as 'a fashionable gathering or assembly, a large evening party or reception, much in vogue in the eighteenth and early nineteenth centuries'.

15, l. 8 Bruar [...] Glen-More Bruar is a rivulet with spectacular waterfalls in the Atholl district. In Gaelic, *Glen-More* means 'the big glen', and (unsurprisingly) there are several glens of that name in Scotland. Here the reference seems to be to the Forest of Glenmore, which lies a little to the north of Atholl, near the Cairngorm Mountains.

16, ll. 34–36 the Monarch stole away [...] well they knew their man in the opening section of *The Lady of the Lake* the king (James V) is likewise separated from his fellow-huntsmen. However, the plot of *Mador of the Moor* also seems to draw on the family of traditional ballads including 'The Jolly Beggar' (Child 279) and 'The Gaberlunzy-Man'. This ballad narrative tells how a beggar, visiting a farm, seduces the family's daughter, and is later revealed to be a rich gentleman. See also Appendix II and this edition's Introduction, p. xxi.

16, l. 55 Ben-Glow Beinn a' Ghlo is a mountain range in Blair Atholl. It rises to a group of five summits, the highest of which is 3671 feet, and is situated to the east of the River Tilt, to the north of the point where the rivers of Atholl join the Tay through the Tummel.

16, l. 58 the heather bell the flower of heather, which grows profusely on the mountains of the Highlands.

17, l. 80 Bayard alludes to the magical legendary horse in medieval chivalric romances. Sometimes the name is used for any horse in a mock-heroic context.

17, l. 81 pathless woods of Dee the River Dee flows east from the Cairngorms to its outlet in the North Sea at Aberdeen. The upper part of its course lies in wild and mountainous country.

17, ll. 91–92 Tilt [...] Tarf the River Tilt begins in the Central Grampians to the north of Atholl, into which it flows. The Tarf is a tributary of the Tilt, which it joins from the west.

17, l. 97 Breriach's at 4248 feet, Breriach is one of the tallest peaks in the Cairngorm Mountains, which are situated in the Central Grampians immediately to the north of Atholl. It lies north and west of Ben Macdui (4296 feet), the highest of the Cairngorms.

17, l. 98 Athol forest's formidable bound the wild and formidable Cairngorms bound Atholl to the north.

17, l. 99 Garcharye one of the two burns or streams which come together to form the River Dee in the Cairngorms.

18, l. 101 Jowler a traditional name for a hound. In a note on 66. 27–28 in his edition of Scott's *The Fortunes of Nigel* (EEWN, 2004), Frank Jordan records that the huntsmen's hounds are called 'Ringwood, Royster, Bowman, Jowler' at l. 51 of 'Old Tom of Bedlam' in Thomas Percy's *Reliques of Ancient English Poetry*. Jordan adds that 'Jowler' was the name of one of the favourite hounds of James VI and I, and that a list of hounds 'naming "Roman and Joller, Ringwood and his mate", occurred in some doggerel verses "found in the hand of Queen Elizabeth's effigy on her tomb in the Abbey"'.

18, l. 109 Macduich's a reference to Ben Macdui: see note on 17, l. 97.

18, ll. 118–35 But O what bard [...] down the broken steep for a discussion of the Miltonic echoes in this passage see this edition's Introduction, pp. xxvii–xxviii.

19, ll. 163–64 that spot [...] memorial of his name although the action has now moved north to the Cairngorms, Hogg here is perhaps bringing in a reference to the Kinnaird area. The village of Logierait ('Gael. *lag-an-rath*, "hollow of the castle"': Groome) lies close to the confluence of the rivers Tay and Tummel, immediately to the north of Kinnaird and Kincraigy. At Logierait, 'a neighbouring eminence was crowned by a castle of Robert III. (1890–1406), and now is the site of a conspicuous and richly-sculptured Celtic cross, erected in 1866 to the memory of the sixth Duke of Athole' (Groome: Robert III was the son of Robert II and Elizabeth Moore or Mure: see note on 5, Advertisement). Robert III used his castle at Logierait as a base for hunting in Atholl. William Marshall comments on 'extant memorials of the honour which Royalty did Logierait in olden times. We have them in names borne by places in the neighbourhood; in Bal-na-guard, the town of the guards; in Rathan-an-righ, the King's road; in the King's stables; and in Canonbrae' (William Marshall, *Historic Scenes in Perthshire* (Edinburgh: Oliphant, 1880), p. 162).

19, l. 168 the Stuart an apt reference for James V as well as for Robert II, both being Stuart kings: cf. Introduction, p. xxi. Robert II was the first Stuart king, inheriting the Scottish throne through his mother Marjorie, daughter of Robert I (the Bruce). The Princess Marjorie was married to Walter the Steward (hence 'Stuart' or 'Stewart').

19, l. 169–70 how unlike the bland voluptuous frame | In this unthrifty age possibly a veiled reference to the luxury-loving and unathletic Prince Regent of the 1810s (later George IV). If so, the contrast with 'the Stuart' in l. 168 can be seen as setting up a hint of a Jacobite resonance.

20, ll. 175–98 wand'ring elfins sly [...] bristle all with fear for a discussion of the echoes of Pope's *The Rape of the Lock* in this passage, see this edition's Introduction, pp. xxv–xxvi.

21, l. 228 Glen-Avin, and the woods of Mar the River Dee (see note on 17, l. 81) flows through the Forest of Mar as it leaves the southern slopes of the Cairngorms before flowing east in the direction of Braemar. Glen Avon is the wild mountain valley of the River Avon, which rises in the Cairngorms a little to the north-east of the source of the Dee. The Avon flows north into the Spey, and thence into the Moray Firth. Glen Avon is the setting for 'Glen-Avin', the first poem of 'Night the Second' in *Hogg's The Queen's Wake* (1813). Hogg had visited this area in 1802, and it seems to have made a strong impression on him: see H. B. de Groot, 'The Unpublished Conclusion of Hogg's 1802 Highland Journey', *SHW*, 6 (1995), 55–66.

21, l. 236 Knight of Souden there is a verbal echo here of Child 305C, the version of the traditional ballad 'The Outlaw Murray' held among the papers collectively called 'Scotch Ballads, Materials for Border Minstrelsy', part of the collections in Scott's library at Abbotsford. This version of the ballad is in the handwriting of Hogg's friend William Laidlaw (Child V, 197). Hogg had supplied information about this ballad to Laidlaw, for onward transmission to Scott: see Edith C. Batho, *The Ettrick Shepherd*

(Cambridge: Cambridge University Press, 1927), pp. 18–19, 177. Stanza 5 in Laidlaw's manuscript reads:

> 'Outlaw Murray says yon land's his ain,
>   And to yon men he pays meat and fee;
> I took it frae the Souden Turk,
>   When you and your men durstna come and see.'

Scott's published version reads 'Frae Soudron I this Foreste wan', and *Soudron* is glossed as 'Southern' or English.

22, l. 261 A visitant [...] from some unhallow'd shrine the events that will flow from this vengeful spirit's haunting of the Knight of Souden draw on a real incident about which Hogg had previously written: see note on 28–29, ll. 488–523, below.

22, l. 268 Gilbert of Sheil Hogg appears to have used the fictional name of Gilbert of Sheil to celebrate the talents of another shepherd minstrel. A *sheil* is a roughly-made hut for shepherds on high ground.

22, l. 275 some fairy isle amid the sea in the Gaelic mythology of the Highlands, fairyland was conceived as 'a mystic green island that drifted on the western seas. Men caught occasional glimpses of it, half hidden in a twinkling mist, but when they attempted to draw near, it vanished beneath the waves. From the island, fairy women came out in magic boats to spirit away those mortals who had won their love, or to convey a dying hero, like Arthur, to Paradise' (see *The Silver Bough*, I, 102–03).

23 The Harper's Song for discussion of 'The Harper's Song' see this edition's Introduction (pp. xxxvii–xxxviii) and Appendix I (pp. 87–95).

23, l. 281 *Lemedon! lemedon! ayden lillelu!* see 'Hind Horn' (Child 17D), taken from R. H. Cromek's *Select Scottish [sic] Songs, Ancient and Modern; with Critical Observations and Biographical Notices by Robert Burns*, 2 vols (London: Cadell and Davies, 1810), II, 204–06, where it appears as 'Young Hynhorn'. In Child stanza 1 reads:

> Near Edinburgh was a young son born,
>   Hey lilelu an a how low lan
> An his name it was called young Hyn Horn.
>   An it's hey down down deedle airo

This song was very much alive in the oral tradition during Hogg's time. Likewise the traditional ballad 'The Maid and the Palmer' (Child 21) has a refrain 'Lillumwham, lillumwham!'.

23, l. 282 his hayre was the woo perhaps an echo of St John's vision of the risen Christ: 'His head and *his* hairs *were* white like wool, as white as snow; and his eyes *were* as a flame of fire' (Revelation 1. 14).

23, l. 283 *Sing Ho! Ro! Gillan of Allanhu!* perhaps an echo of 'Roderigh Vich Alpine dhu, ho! iero!', the chorus in the 'Boat Song' in Canto II of *The Lady of the Lake*.

23, l. 287 Lammer Law at 1733 feet, Lammer Law is the highest of the Lammermuir Hills, which lie within East Lothian and Berwickshire in the Scottish Borders.

23, l. 291 neuir his lene never alone.

23, l. 299 damyske roz according to the *OED*, the 'damask rose' is 'a species or variety of rose, supposed to have been brought from Damascus'. The word 'damask' is used to describe the 'blush' colour of this rose and, poetically, the blush of a woman's cheek: cf. *Twelfth Night*, II. 4. 110.

23, ll. 310–11 neuir agayne | Shalt' heire sikn wylde wanyirdlye strayne the departure of the fairies also features in Hogg's poem 'Superstition', in which he writes (addressing Superstition): 'Long did thy fairies linger in the wild, | When vale and city wholly were resigned': the mountains 'were their last retreats, and heard their parting strain' (see Hogg, *The Pilgrims of the Sun* (Edinburgh: Blackwood; London: Murray, 1815), pp. 138–39). See also Hogg's poems 'The Origin of the Fairies' and 'The Last Stork' in *A Queer Book*, ed. Garside (S/SC, 1995), pp. 157–69 and 180–88. Hogg's maternal grandfather Will Laidlaw was reputed to be the last man in Ettrick 'who heard, saw, and conversed with the fairies': see Hogg, *The Shepherd's Calendar*, ed. by Douglas S. Mack (S/SC, 1995), p. 107.

24, l. 323 Fayrie-land in contrast to the Gaelic Highland tradition (see note on 22, l. 275) the fairyland of Hogg's native Lowland tradition was 'a subterranean land entered through a cavern or hill, and thither, as we read in the ballads [for example 'Thomas Rymer', Child 37], the Queen of Elfhame, mounted on her milk-white steed, carried off those mortals on whom she had cast her spell' (see *The Silver Bough*, I, 102–03). Hogg's view of fairies and fairyland is further influenced by associations from Shakespeare and Spenser.

24, l. 326 Quhyte [...] Blak presumably 'black' magic and its opposite 'white' magic, black magic being 'the kind of magic that was supposed to involve the invocation of devils': see *OED* under *Magic*.

24, l. 330 blever blue the harebell (Scottish bluebell), a plant with blue bell-shaped flowers: see *SND* under *blue-bell*.

24, l. 347 Laplin's Lapland is a region in northern Europe composed of northern Norway, northern Sweden, northern Finland, and the Kola Peninsula of the northwestern portion of Russia. In *The Queen's Wake* (1813) the witches of 'The Witch of Fife' go to Lapland for their revels.

24, ll. 350–51 Our hune! hune! | And ante-tune perhaps refers to *tone* and *antiphon* in plainsong: *tone* signifies any of the nine plainsong psalm-tunes, while *antiphon* signifies 'a short piece of plain-song introduced before a psalm or canticle, to the Tone of which it corresponds, while the words are selected so as specially to illustrate and enforce the evangelical or prophetic meaning of the text' (see *OED*).

24, l. 353 Up the Leider and doune the Dye Leader Water and Dye Water are streams of the Lammermuirs (cf. note on 23, l. 287). Dye Water rises about two miles from Lammer Law. Under *Leader Water*, Groome records that this stream rises 'as Kelhope Burn at an altitude of 1375 feet on the southern slope of Lammer Law', and joins the Tweed about two miles east of Melrose.

25, l. 365 quhan the sone keikes out of the maine the Lammermuirs are on the east coast of Scotland, so from these hills the morning sun is seen to rise from the sea (the main).

25, l. 393 Gil-Moules Hogg used 'Gil-Moules' as a name for the Devil in various works: see *The Private Memoirs and Confessions of a Justified Sinner*, ed. by P. D. Garside (S/SC, 2001), p. xiv.

27, l. 440 the emerant isle of the se in 'Superstition and Grace' (see this edition's Appendix I) this becomes 'the queen isle of the sea' (that is, Imperial Britain).

28–29, ll. 488–523 At midnight, strange disturbing sounds [...] and deep unseemly wound the account of the destruction of the hunters, which appears in stanzas 37–40, has a prose original in 'Dreadful Narrative of the Death of Major MacPherson', in no. 13 of *The Spy*, 24 November 1810, pp. 101–03. Various details in the poem are matched by this narrative, which is based on a real incident that took place in January 1800 at Gaick, which lies among the mountains of Atholl above Dalnacardoch, a little to the south-west of the Cairngorms. At Gaick, Captain John Macpherson and members of his shooting party were killed by an avalanche as they sheltered in a forest hut: see Roger Leitch, 'Hogg, Scott, and the Gaick Catastrophe', *SHW*, 1 (1990), 126–28. Leitch comments (pp. 126–27) that Gaik already had a 'demon-haunted reputation', and the incident entered local folklore. Hogg's account in *The Spy* seems to have been based on an oral source, presumably encountered when he visited Dalnacardoch in July 1802. Leitch continues:

> Hogg states that Macpherson 'was said to have been guilty of some acts of extreme cruelty and injustice in raising recruits in that country, and was, on that account, held in detestation by the common people'. [...] According to Hogg's version, earlier in the week that the tragedy occurred, Macpherson had visited Gaick and there he had encountered a mysterious stranger who seemed to threaten him before making a spectre-like exit. This greatly disturbed Macpherson and altered the entire mood of the hunting party. The reader is left with the conclusion that this was a ghost. By the Friday immediately following, a second expedition to Gaick was proposed despite uncertain weather. 'Those who did not chuse to accompany him, might tarry at home'. All but one decided to follow. None returned, bar a solitary dog who was wounded and maimed. (p. 127)

29, ll. 529–31 Moulin [...] nine rude stones Moulin is a village in Perthshire, near Pitlochry. Groome records (under *Moulin*) that Moulin parish contains 'Caledonian standing-stones, Druidical circles, Pictish forts, and sites of pre-reformation burying-grounds'.

29, l. 538 Saint Bothan's shrine may be a reference to Saint Bathan or Bothanus, who has been associated with various places in Scotland. He is one of the addressees of a letter of Pope John IV (640) on the Easter question and the danger of Pelagianism. See David Hugh Farmer, *The Oxford Dictionary of Saints* (Oxford: Clarendon Press, 1978), under *Bathan*.

Canto Second: The Minstrel

31 Argument these lines derive from the chorus of a popular broadside *The Taylor of Hogerglen's Wedding* (1776: see Ritter, *Neue Quellenfunde*, 1903, pp. 23–25). Burns retained the chorus while revising the song into 'The Taylor' (Kinsley, 586).

33, l. 4 honest as a Highlander may be reflects the traditional Lowland stereotype, in which the Highlander is seen as feckless and dishonest.

34, l. 31 Albert of the Glen the name of this character was perhaps suggested to Hogg by a local placename: Glenalbert lies about three-quarters of a mile south of Kincraigy (see note on 35, l. 68).

34, ll. 55–57 O fragile flower! [...] walk'st the dizzy verge this passage seems to refer to and echo 'On the Death of a Favourite Cat, Drowned in a Tub of Goldfishes', by Thomas Gray (1716–71). Hogg echoes Gray in having a female figure (woman / cat) leaning over a tempting but dangerous brink (in Gray, the cat is tempted by goldfish in a bowl). Both passages are cautionary: a woman who falls cannot be reinstated to virtue. As Gray's poem puts it, 'one false step is ne'er retrieved'.

34, ll. 58–59 **Fair as the habitants of yonder skies! | Like them, thou fallest never more to rise** a reference to Lucifer's fallen angels.

35, l. 66 **Ila Moore** for Elizabeth ('Ila') Moore, see Introduction (p. xxi) and the note for 5 Advertisement.

35, l. 68 **Kincraigy** following standard Scottish practice, Hogg uses this term variously to refer to the farmhouse in which some of the action of the poem takes place, to the cluster of cottages surrounding the farmhouse, and to the the farmer of Kincraigy, the father of Ila Moore. A farmhouse at Kincraigy still overlooks the Tay to the north of Dunkeld. Part of the Kinnaird estate, Kincraigy is near Kinnaird House where Hogg reportedly wrote *Mador of the Moor*.

35, l. 91 **ashen board** a table made of ashwood, an inferior, softer, and less expensive wood than would be found in a more prosperous home.

35, l. 96 **Mador of the Moor** for a discussion of the name 'Mador', see the Introduction at pp. xxxix–xl.

36, l. 113 **rocket Minstrel** 'rocket' in this context suggests 'moving with manic energy' (cf. stanza 10).

37, l. 145 **Cairn-Gorm** Cairn Gorm Mountain (4084 feet) is one of the peaks in the Cairngorm Mountains, north of Glen Lynn.

37, l. 146 **Schehallion** a mountain (3547 feet) north of Loch Tay: see also note on 45, l. 443.

40, l. 264 **parting rivers** the confluence of the Tay and the Tummel near Logierait (see note on 19, ll. 163–64) lies just to the north of Kincraigy, and the various rivers of Atholl join the Tay through the Tummel. The Tummel joins the Tay from the east, while Kincraigy is on the Tay's west bank. Mador therefore has to cross the Tay in order to return to Atholl.

40, l. 278 **'Twas but one little mile!—a summer day** because of Scotland's northern latitude, daylight is very long-lasting there during the summer.

43, l. 358 **An ancient Friar, who shrived the family** this emphasises the pre-Reformation, medieval setting of the poem—a setting appropriate to the reigns of both Robert II and James V (see Introduction, p. xxi).

43, l. 365 **frock of gray** Franciscans were called 'grey friars' because of the colour of their clothing.

43, l. 368 **wells of Dee** the source of the River Dee in the Cairngorms.

44, l. 400 **No ruthless abbey reave, nor Ranoch thief** the reeve of a pre-Reformation abbey would have the task of overseeing the abbey's estates and tenants, and *reave* was a possible spelling of *reeve* in the sixteenth and seventeenth centuries. Hogg puns here on *reave*, 'to rob': to those he pesters for contributions, a reeve can appear to be a reaver. Rannoch Loch lies in the Grampian Mountains. A seventeenth-century observer, Sir John Dalrymple of Stair (1648–1707), called the MacDonalds of Glencoe the worst thieves in the Highlands. They were reputed to operate around the River Orchy, across the moor of Rannoch: see Rosalind Mitchison, *A History of Scotland*, (London: Methuen, 1970), p. 187.

45, l. 431 she had sung beneath the willow tree there is a suggestion here of the phrase 'to wear the willow', that is, to bewail a lost lover. See *Othello* IV. 3. 25–27: 'My mother had a maid called Barbary. | She was in love, and he she loved proved mad | And did forsake her. She had a song of willow'. There is also an echo of Psalm 137. 1–3: 'By the rivers of Babylon, there we sat down, yea, we wept, when we remembered Zion. We hanged our harps upon the willows in the midst thereof. For there they that carried us away captive required of us a song'.

45, l. 443 fairy mound that overlooks the Tay 'it is doubtful if there is a parish in Scotland which did not once possess at least one fairy hill, although these are being gradually forgotten; and in addition there was in every region a larger hill where fairies from far and wide foregathered on the eve of the Quarter Days and other high occasions. Among the most famous are Tom-na-hurich in Inverness; the Fairy Hill of Aberfoyle; the Calton Hill, in Edinburgh; and the Eildon Hills, in the Borders, whither Thomas the Rhymer was lured by the Fairy Queen [see Child 37]; and if ever our Scottish fairies held a National Mod [that is, a Gaelic festival of music and poetry], the site was surely that Grampian peak, Schiehallion (Gael. *Sìdh Chailleann*) [see note on 37, l. 146], the Fairy Hill of the Caledonians' (*The Silver Bough*, I, 108–09).

45, l. 444 Kinnaird Hogg refers to Kinnaird House which is adjacent to Kincraigy. Kinnaird House was the home of the Chalmers Izett family, and Hogg claims to have begun *Mador of the Moor* while a guest there. During 1823–24, Thomas Carlyle wrote most of his life of Schiller and prepared the first part of his translation of *Wilhelm Meister* while serving as tutor to the Bullers, who were tenants there at this later date. After undergoing several additions and modifications in the more than two hundred years since Hogg visited, Kinnaird House, now an elegant country hotel, again welcomes guests and visitors.

46, l. 471 Mador of the Moor, o'erborne at last in *The Lady of the Lake* the disguised king cuts a much more heroic figure: he fights and wins a single combat against a Highland chief.

Canto Third. The Cottage

49 Argument these eight lines are taken from the old traditional song 'Waly, Waly, Gin Love be Bonny': see the introductory note to Child 204 'Jamie Douglas', in which this old song is reprinted from Allan Ramsay's *Tea-Table Miscellany*. 'Waly, Waly' is a song of love betrayed.

51, l. 23 crazing bowl that is, 'maddening drinking vessel'.

52, ll. 37–45 Then speed, thou great coeval of the sun; […] to yon eternal shore these lines are a revision of the third stanza of Hogg's poem 'To Time', published in no. 43 of *The Spy* (22 June 1811): see *The Spy*, ed. Hughes (S/SC, 2000), p. 436.

52, l. 57 lovely Ila, by the aged thorn a reference to the ballad of 'The Cruel Mother', Child 20: 'she leaned her back against a thorn'. This motif, which also appears in *Mador* at Canto III l. 8, is commonly used in traditional ballads to signal pregnancy and childbirth. 'The Cruel Mother' is one of the sources of Wordsworth's well-known poem 'The Thorn' (from *Lyrical Ballads*), and Hogg would have been familiar with both 'The Cruel Mother' and 'The Thorn'. For 'The Cruel Mother', which connects significantly with

Mador of the Moor in various ways, see this edition's Appendix II.

55, ll. 154–62 Poor child of shame! [...] cradled on guileless breast the eighteenth-century country people among whom Hogg grew up tended to take a relaxed view of illegitimacy, although the official church view was more severe, and attitudes became more censorious in the nineteenth century. Hogg's attitudes to this matter (both in his life and in his writings, and not least in *The Three Perils of Woman*) are discussed in Gillian Hughes's important article, 'James Hogg and the "Bastard Brood"', *SHW*, 11 (2000), 56–68. Hughes concludes (p. 66): 'In its treatment of sexual morality *The Three Perils of Woman* is both a profoundly Christian and a profoundly radical work, and it is hardly surprising that in the increasingly squeamish pre-Victorian world of the 1820s it was widely regarded as an immoral one. If illegitimate children were the "bastard brood" to William Blackwood, to James Hogg they were always primarily children'.

55, l. 161 Unhousell'd this word means 'not having had the Eucharist administered', but Hogg (mistakenly) seems to use it to mean 'unchristened'.

56, ll. 174–76 th' unchristen'd babe [...] malignant elves it was believed that an unchristened baby was unprotected against fairy power; and that the fairies might steal such a child, leaving a changeling behind. According to *The Silver Bough* 'new-born children were in especial danger, and young mothers would not go out after dark until the christening was over, when the fairy power became ineffective'; without special protective rites 'the child might be spirited away, and in its place would be left a puny, peevish changeling, which would slowly dwine away and die' (pp. 113–14). See also Suzanne Gilbert, 'Hogg's "Kilmeny" and the Ballad of Supernatural Abduction', *SHW*, 8 (1997), 42–55.

56, ll. 205–06 the unrighteous babe, [...] from saints' society difficulties could arise over the baptism of an illegitimate child. In Hogg's *Justified Sinner* (1824) the possibily illegitimate Robert Wringhim has to remain for a time unbaptised, 'an alien from the visible church': see *The Private Memoirs and Confessions of a Justified Sinner*, ed. by P. D. Garside (S/SC, 2001), p. 14.

Canto Fourth. The Palmer

59 Argument a source for these lines has not been located: they may be Hogg's invention.

61, l. 7 That broken reed, Dependence the phrase is proverbial (see *ODEP*), p. 88. It derives from II Kings 18. 21: 'Now, behold, thou trustest upon the staff of this bruised reed, even upon Egypt, on which if a man lean, it will go into his hand, and pierce it: so is Pharaoh king of Egypt unto all that trust on him'.

61, l. 25 With robe of green, upfolded to her knee an echo of the ballad 'Tam Lin' (Child 39): 'Janet has kilted her green kirtle | A little aboon her knee'. This is an apt echo because, like Isla Moore, the Janet of the ballad becomes pregnant out of wedlock and takes decisive action to become reunited with her lover. 'Tam Lin' is set in the Ettrick valley, and seems to have been an important ballad for Hogg: it is sung by the Bard of Ettrick (Hogg's representative) in the concluding stages of *The Queen's Wake* (1813).

62, l. 28 woods of Bran this reference is to the wooded regions surrounding the River Braan which rises to the south of Loch Tay and joins the Tay at Dunkeld.

63, l. 71 Elfin King th' unchristened babe had won see note on 56, ll. 174–76.

63, l. 74 Would change to something of unearthly guise another echo of 'Tam Lin' (see note on 61, l. 25). To rescue her lover from the fairy Queen, Janet has to cling to him as he goes through a series of horrifying transformations.

64, ll. 122–26 He, who deign'd to feed | The plumeless sea-bird [...] to sorrow and to pain echoes a passage from Christ's Sermon on the Mount: 'Therefore I say unto you, Take no thought for your life, what ye shall eat, or what ye shall drink; nor yet for your body, what ye shall put on. Is not the life more than meat, and the body than raiment? Behold the fowls of the air: for they sow not, neither do they reap, nor gather into barns; yet your heavenly father feedeth them. Are ye not much better than they?' (Matthew 6. 25–26).

65, l. 170 Whether through glamour or bewilder'd thought *glamour* is used here in its original Scottish sense of 'magic, enchantment, witchcraft'.

66 The Palmer's Morning Hymn shortly before his death Hogg recycled 'The Palmer's Morning Hymn' as a contribution ('Morning Hymn') to the annual *The Amulet* for 1836, pp. 42–43.

66, l. 184 Till the last lingering sand of night was run in an hourglass, the period of time being measured has expired when the 'last lingering sand' runs out.

67, l. 215 Thou, who slumber'st not, nor sleepest an echo of Psalm 121. 3–4. For Lowland Scots of Hogg's social and cultural background, this Psalm has long been a particular favourite, especially in the Church of Scotland's metrical version, in which the relevant passage reads: 'Thy foot he'll not let slide, nor will | he slumber that thee keeps. | Behold, he that keeps Israel, | he slumbers not, nor sleeps'.

67, l. 238 the emerald gates of Heaven perhaps a reference to Revelation 4. 1–3.

68, l. 249 Almond the Almond River rises in Perthshire, near Loch Tay, and joins the Tay north of Perth.

68, ll. 264–65 No plaint of thy just wounds be heard to flow, | The hand that gave will bind them up again echoes Hosea 6. 1–2: 'Come, and let us return unto the Lord: for he hath torn, and he will heal us; he hath smitten, and he will bind us up. After two days will he revive us; in the third day he will raise us up, and we shall live in his sight'. In the Christian tradition this famous Old Testament passage has sometimes been thought to prefigure Christ's resurrection. Metrical 'Paraphrases' of Biblical passages are traditionally sung in the worship of the Church of Scotland, and Hogg would certainly have been familiar with one of the most famous of these, Paraphrase 30, which is based on Hosea 6. 1–4. Paraphrase 30 connects in various ways with the concerns of Canto IV of *Mador of the Moor*. It reads in part:

> Long hath the night of sorrow reign'd;
>   the dawn shall bring us light:
> God shall appear, and we shall rise
>   with gladness in his sight.
> Our hearts, if God we seek to know,

shall know him, and rejoice;
His coming like the morn shall be,
like morning songs his voice

68–70, ll. 267–347 "I was the lord of Stormont's fertile bound, [...] I must go pray to God, for I am rack'd and torn!" the Palmer's tale of his own perfidy is based on the ballad 'The Cruel Mother' (Child 20). For the relationship between *Mador of the Moor* and 'The Cruel Mother', see note on 52, l. 57, and this edition's Appendix II. Stormont is an extensive district in Perthshire, bounded on the east by the Ericht, on the south by the Isla and the Tay, on the west by the Tay, and on the north by the lower Highlands.

68, l. 268 Isla's vale, and Eroch's woodland glade Eroch is probably a rendering of Ericht. The River Isla rises in the Grampians, and joins the Tay at a point that lies about ten miles upstream from Perth, and about thirteen miles downstream from Kincraigy. It is joined by the Ericht two miles north-east of Coupar Angus.

68, l. 271 proud Matilda Hogg assigns the name of Matilda to the young woman whom the Palmer once loved. 'Matilda of Skye' is the Abbot's lover in 'The Abbot M'Kinnon', the concluding song in *The Queen's Wake* (1813).

69, ll. 278–79 she appear'd the gayest maid to be | That graced the hall, or gambol'd at the play 'The Cruel Mother' has 'She's aff untill her father's ha; | She was the lealest maiden that was amang them a' (Child 20D).

69, l. 280 Methven's lord Methven, a village in Perthshire, lies a few miles east of Perth, near the River Almond.

69, l. 288 a shining row of children small here, and in what follows, 'The Cruel Mother' is again being closely paralleled.

69, l. 304 if thou wert mine 'The Cruel Mother' has: 'O sweet babe, and thou were mine, | I wad cleed thee in the silk so fine' (Child 20B).

70, l. 345 name me crazy Connel of the hill Hogg may have in mind the eponymous hero of his poem 'Connel of Dee', written around the same time as *Mador*: see 'Memoir' p. 35, and Hogg, *Winter Evening Tales*, ed. by Ian Duncan (S/SC, 2002), pp. 400–25, 582.

71, l. 376 Strathallan the vale of Strathallan runs from the northeast to the southwest between Gleneagles and Dunblane, just north of Stirling, near the boundary between the Highlands and the Lowlands. It forms part of the natural route to Stirling from the Tay in the vicinity of Perth.

Canto Fifth: The Christening

73 Argument the first lines of the Argument derive from the traditional ballad 'Child Maurice' (Child 83E), in which a child's identity is questioned and finally revealed. The formulaic silk/milk construction of the second part occurs in several other ballads that involve revelations of identity, among them 'Gil Brenton' (Child 5) and a variant of it called 'Cospatrick' that appeared in Scott's *Minstrelsy*; 'Willie o Douglas Dale' (Child 101A); and 'Child Waters' (Child 63).

75, l. 1 Strevline [...] beauteous on the height 'Strevline' is an early term for Stirling. The oldest part of the town sits near Stirling Castle, on a high crag overlooking fertile plains and the River Forth, with mountains beyond.

75, l. 3 bewilder'd waves of silvery light immediately downstream from Stirling the River Forth enters a spectacular series of meanders. The river is tidal at this point, and below Stirling it gradually expands into the Firth of Forth, the broad inlet from the North Sea on which Edinburgh lies.

75, ll. 11–12 martial towers [...] mouldering palaces one of the palaces of the Scottish monarchy formed part of the strongly fortified Stirling Castle.

75, ll. 14–15 when hostile powers | So often proved thy stedfast patriot worth famous Scottish victories over invading English armies were won within sight of Stirling Castle by William Wallace (Stirling Bridge, 1297) and Robert I (Bannockburn, 1314).

75, l. 17 Forth see note on 75, l. 3.

75, l. 18 old bulwark of the North Stirling's strategic importance lay in the fact that it was for centuries the lowest point on the river Forth at which there was a bridge. For this reason, it commanded the natural route for an army moving between northern and southern Scotland.

76, l. 46 wander'd round the rock Stirling Castle is built on a clifftop site on the massive Castle Rock.

77, l. 64 Abbot of Dunfermline Dunfermline lies a few miles north of the Firth of Forth across from Edinburgh. When the Scottish kings lost their ancient burial site of Iona to the Norse, they were buried in the new Benedictine abbey in Dunfermline.

78, l. 125 up the hill that is, towards the castle and the palace.

80, l. 189 The knight is Mador hight the Abbot confronts the king with his guilt in a way closely modelled on II Samuel 12. 1–13, in which the prophet Nathan confronts King David with regard to the king's seduction of Bathsheba (subsequently David's queen).

81, ll. 226–34 When from the chamber [...] form'd thee for a queen an echo of the ballad 'The Jolly Beggar (Child 279): for this ballad see note on 16, ll. 34–36 and Appendix II. Here Isla's queenly nature is revealed when she appears in rich clothes, while in the ballad the real nature of the Jolly Beggar / James V is similarly revealed: 'And he took out his little knife, loot a' his duddies fa' | And he was the brawest gentleman that was amang them a'' (Child 279B, stanza 13).

82, l. 270 all thy native hills, from Tay to Bran the River Bran, or Braan, issues from Loch Freuchie, east of Loch Tay, and joins the Tay at Dunkeld. Kincraigy is situated on the mountainous land which lies between the rivers Tay and Braan.

83, ll. 284–86 a lowly spot [...] our cot shall be Hogg seems to have the site of Robert III's hunting-seat at Logierait near Kinnaird in mind for the location of the the rural retreat of Mador and Ila: see notes on 5 Advertisement; 19, ll. 163–64; and 40, l. 264.

83, l. 289 silken screen suggests a gossamer fabric which diffuses light.

83, l. 300 gold and scarlet the colours of the standard of the Kings of Scots (the lion rampant).

83, ll. 310–13 All who have heard of maid of low degree, [...] May well conceive who Mador needs must be a reference to the 'incident recorded in the Scottish annals of the 14th century' mentioned in the Advertisement (p. 5): see also the note on 5 Advertisement.

Conclusion

85, l. 1 RETURN, my Harp, unto the Border dale a reference to Hogg's most famous and recently-written poem, *The Queen's Wake* (1813), which likewise ends with an address by the poet to his harp. In *The Queen's Wake* Hogg's harp (that is to say, his poetic inspiration) is strongly identified with his native Borders.

85, l. 2 Thy native green hill, and thy fairy ring this perhaps connects with the subject-matter of Hogg's 'mountain an' fairy' school of poetry: see Introduction, p. xxxi.

85, l. 7 Ossian in Gaelic legend, Ossian is a hero and poet who is supposed to have lived during the third century A.D. In the eighteenth century, James Macpherson, capitalising on the popular interest in simple and naive verse, pursued fame by writing imitations of Ossian's poems. Ossian was often pictured playing a harp. Like many of his contemporaries, Hogg was strongly aware of Macpherson's *Ossian* poems: see Valentina Bold, 'The Mountain Bard: James Hogg and Macpherson's Ossian', *SHW*, 9 (1998), 32–44.

85, l. 10 Loved was the voice the part played by Eliza Izett in the genesis of *Mador of the Moor* is discussed in the Introduction.

85, l. 10 Yarrow a parish in Selkirkshire, is bounded for a few miles by Yarrow Water. Hogg lived much of his adult life in the Yarrow valley in the Scottish Borders not far from Ettrick. The valley was celebrated in many traditional ballads and became a literary topic in William Wordsworth's poems 'Yarrow Unvisited (1803), 'Yarrow Visited' (1814) and 'Yarrow Revisited' (1831).

85, l. 20 Although proud learning lift the venom'd eye Hogg's strength of feeling on this subject also emerges in the 'Memoir' (p. 46):

> For my own part, I know that I have always been looked on by the learned part of the community as an intruder in the paths of litera-ture, and every opprobrium has been thrown on me from that quar-ter. The truth is, that I am so. The walks of learning are occupied by a powerful aristocracy, who deem that province their own peculiar right; else, what would avail all their dear-bought collegiate honours and degrees? No wonder that they should view an intruder, from the humble and despised ranks of the community, with a jealous and indignant eye, and impede his progress by every means in their power.

85, l. 27 by other hands *The Queen's Wake* (1813) is set in the sixteenth century at the court of Mary, Queen of Scots, and in that poem Hogg presents himself as the successor of a sixteenth-century 'Bard of Ettrick'. Here Hogg is asserting that the poetic tradition of the people of Ettrick, a tradition that he himself inherited and continued, will be in turn inherited and continued by others, after his own time.

Glossary

The aim of this Glossary is to provide a convenient guide to unfamiliar words and orthographical variants in *Mador of the Moor*. The focus here is on single words; explanations of phrases, expressions, and idioms may be found in the Notes. In interpreting Hogg's mock-antique Scots in 'The Harper's Song' it is important to remember that 'quh-' is the equivalent of 'wh-' and '-it' is the equivalent of '-ed'; and that plurals can take the form '-is' rather than '-s'. Mock-antique words that appear in 'The Harper's Song' in unfamiliar but readily recognisable form are generally not included in the Glossary. For further elucidation of 'The Harper's Song' see this edition's Appendix I; and for serious study of Hogg's use of Scots, see *The Concise Scots Dictionary*, ed. by Mairi Robinson (Aberdeen: Aberdeen University Press, 1985), and *The Scottish National Dictionary*, ed. by William Grant and David Murison, 10 vols (Edinburgh: Scottish National Dictionary Association, 1931–76). The present Glossary is much indebted to *The Scottish National Dictionary* (*SND*) and *The Oxford English Dictionary* (*OED*).

a': all
aboone: above
acritude: sharpness or pungency; biting quality
adjudgment: the act of adjudication
affray: an alarm or disturbance
aident: assiduous, conscientious
ain: own
ake: to wake
amain: with full force
anchorite: a recluse or hermit
ante-tune: see note on 24, ll. 350–51
antick: incongruous, grotesque, or ludicrous
arraign: to accuse, to call in question
arrant: thorough, downright, notorious: (used as an intensifier)
asklent: aslant
aspin: an aspen, a kind of poplar tree with especially tremulous leaves
assay: to attempt
asteep: steeped, soaked
avale: to avail; to be of value or profit to
aver: to assert

ay, aye: always
ayden: see note on 23, l. 282
ayril: meaning uncertain, but possibly signifying a musical air

bairn, bairne: a child, either male or female
baited: tormented
baldrick: a belt or girdle usually worn pendent from one shoulder across the breast and under the opposite arm and used to support the wearer's sword or bugle
bane: that which causes death or destruction; a poison
baste: to beat soundly, to thrash
baulk'd: thwarted
bausin'd: spotted or piebald; having a blaze
Bayard: see note on 17, l. 80
bays: a wreath of leaves of the bay tree, worn by conquerors or poets; laurels
bedight: equipped or furnished
beetling: projecting or overhanging

beguiled: foiled or diverted from

behest: a command

behove: to befit

bell: to make the cry of a deer (especially of a stag or buck at rutting time)

beltane: festival which marked the first of May or the beginning of summer

belted: see note on 10, l. 41

benignity: kindness of disposition

beshrew: curse

bespent: exhausted

betray: to cheat

betrothed: engaged to be married

betyde: betide, happen

bewray: to reveal or disclose

birken: birchen, composed of birch

biz: a state of commotion; to buzz

blab: foolish talk

black-cock: the male of the black grouse or black gamecock

bleeter: the common snipe

blench: to make pale

blent: blended

blet: bleated

blever: see note on 24, l. 330

blowzy: coarse, slatternly

blyth: blithe, glad, mirthful

bolised: perhaps relating to *bolide*, a meteor that explodes and falls in the form of aerolites: a fire-ball

bonny, bonnye: comely, beautiful, pleasing to the sight

boon: congenial, jolly

boots: profits or gives advantage

bore: a hole; an opening in the clouds

boreal: northern

bothy: a hut or cottage

bourn: boundary or limit

brae: a steep slope or bank

brake: a thicket

braken: fern

bray: a loud noise

bree: the eyebrow

brindled: tawny with streaks of other colour

brock: a badger

brocket: a stag in its second year with its first horns, which are straight and single, like a small dagger

brook: tolerate or endure or put up with

brume: broom, a yellow-flowered shrub

bught: a sheepfold; more strictly a small pen, usually in the corner of the fold, used for keeping ewes when they were to be milked

builziment: abuilziements, garments

burn: a stream or brook

byde: to remain

cairn: a pile of stones raised as a memorial or marker

cam: came

carl, caryl: a man, a fellow

cerulean: deep blue; the colour of the cloudless sky

chafed: vexed, angered, disturbed

coeval: of equal antiquity; equally old

coil: noisy disturbance or row

con: to study, to learn

condign: merited, severe

cot: a small house or little cottage

couldna: could not

cowl: a garment with a hood, worn by monks

crazing: see note on 51, l. 23

creukis: odd corners, nooks

cronach: a funeral dirge, a lament

cuerlet: coverlet

cumber'd: burdened

damask, damyske: see note on 23, l. 299

deide: dead

dell: a deep natural hollow or vale of no great extent

deray: disorderly revelry

dern: somber, wild, dreary

dernis: hides

dew-bell: a drop of dew

dewlap: the loose skin under the throat of an animal

dight: dressed, arrayed

diske: dusk

dole: grief, woe

doone: a hill

dor-ke: a door-key

dor-threshil: a threshold

doughtna: was not able to, did not have the strength to (strong past tense of *dow* : see *SND*)

doure: stern, severe

dowie: sad, dismal

dowlas: a coarse kind of linen, much used in the 16th and 17th centuries

dowle: perhaps from *doolie*, a hob-goblin

dreid: dread

driver: in a hunt, individuals known as drivers would be charged with creating an ever-narrowing circle, forcing wildlife to congregate at a point near the hunters

dryfte: falling snow driven by the wind

dule: grief, distress

dun: a dull or dingy brown

ee: the eye

eglantine: the sweet-briar

eiless: eyeless

eirye: eerie

eke: also; in addition to

eldrich: weird

elfin: a fairy creature

emerant: emerald

entreatance: entreaty or intercession

erdlich: unearthly

erewhile: before, formerly

erghe: to be timid, to hesitate

erlisch: unearthly

erne: an eagle

erst: formerly

everilke: every

fay: a fairy

fell: fierce, ruthless

fere: a puny, dwarfish person

flaucht: to weave, to intertwine, to link together

flawmand: a history, a narrative (see *SND, flawmont*)

flew: the hanging lip of a blood-hound

flycherynge: fluttering

flytt: to leave a place, to go else-where

forelay: to frustrate, hinder or interfere with

fraught: laden or loaded as a ship filled with cargo

freak: a sudden change of mind; a capricious notion; a trick or prank

frehynde: from behind

frontlet: facade, forehead

froward: perverse, ungovernable, difficult to deal with

fulsome: abundant, plentiful, full

gae: go

gainsay: to deny, to contradict, to speak against

gaire: a strip of green grass on a hillside

gall: to irritate, to chafe, to rub the wrong way; bitterness

geire: clay

gelid: chilling, icy cold

getis: brats

gill: a deep ravine, usually wooded and forming the course of a stream

Gil-Moules: see note on 25, l. 393

gimp: slender, delicate, or graceful

glamour: see note on 65, l. 170

gleid: a spark, a glimmer

gleide: the kite, the buzzard

gloamyng, glomyng: twilight

gor-cock: the male of the red grouse

goud: gold

gowin: the daisy (gowan)

gowl: to howl, to yell, to weep noisily

graved: engraved or carved

guerdon: a reward or recompense

gyis: masquerades

gyre: supernatural

gysand: shrivelled, withered

hallen: a screen erected between the outer door of a cottage and the fireplace to give protection from draughts

hart: a stag; a male deer, especially of the red deer species

hasp: a device for fastening a door or lid; metaphorically, hands encircling the neck of Mador as Albert attempts to strangle the minstrel

heath-cock: the male of the heath-bird or black grouse; in North America, the Canada grouse and other species

herpe: a harp

hiche: high

hie: to make haste, to go quickly

hight: called or named

hind: a female deer; a farm hand, a rustic

hoar: venerable, grey with age

homily: a sermon or religious discourse

houlat: the owl

howe: a hollow, a valley

hune: see note on 24, ll. 350–51

husbandman: a tiller of the soil

hyng: to hang

ill: difficult, troublesome, hard

imbrue: to soak, saturate, or stain

immure: to encircle or to enclose

imp: a mischievous child

incondite: unformed, crude, haphazard

indite: to compose

inurn: to entomb or bury

jars: harsh, inharmonious sounds or combination of sounds

jocosely: playfully

jolliment: mirth or merriment

keel: the lowest longitudinal timber of a ship on which the framework is built

keike: to peep, to glance

kelpye: a water demon, a kelpie

ken: knowledge or understanding

kend: knew

keust: cast, threw

klaiver: clover

kythe: to show, to reveal, to make manifest

lak: a flow

lang: long

larum: alarm or uproar

laueroke: the skylark

lay: a short lyric or narrative poem intended to be sung

le, lee: a tract of open ground

leifu: compassionate, lovely

leil: loyal, faithful, or honest

lemedon: see note on 23, l. 282

leuer: a gleam, a faint ray

libbert: meaning uncertain

liege: the superior to whom one owes feudal allegiance or services

liegeman: a faithful follower or vassal

lieve: gladly (as in 'as lief')

lillelu: a lullaby, a refrain; see also note on 23, l. 282

links: the windings of a stream, or the land enclosed by these windings

linn: a precipice or ravine

loan: open place where cows are milked

loth: disinclined

lour: to look threatening or gloomy

luias: hallelujahs

lychte: light

lyfte: the sky, the heavens

lyng: to swing along

lynkis: the windings of a stream, or the land enclosed by these windings

mace: a heavy staff or club

maine: see note on 25, l. 365

marten: a weasel-like animal, yielding a valuable fur

matin: morning song

maune: must

may: a young woman

mean: undistinguished in position, rank, or station

meed: reward or recompense

meikle: great in bulk, stature, or size

mene: must

mene: a moan

meridian: mid-day or noon

merl: the blackbird

merlin: a merlin, a falcon

merlit: marled

mer-mayde: a mermaid

mien: the bearing or carriage of a person; appearance

mochte: might

moon-rak: clouds around the moon (moon-rack)

moote: to mutter in a discontented manner

morion: a kind of helmet, without beaver or visor

muckle: great in bulk, stature, or size

mure: moor

musk-rose: a rambling rose, having large, fragrant white flowers

no: not

nychte-gale: a nightingale

obsequies: funeral rites or ceremonies

orisons: prayers

osprey: a large diurnal bird of prey frequenting rocky seashores

ouph: a goblin child (see *OED* under *ouph* and *auf*)

ouphen: elfin, consisting of goblin children

overlay: an outer garment

palfrey: saddle-horse for ordinary riding

pall: literally, the cloth covering a coffin; figuratively, a cloud of gloom

palmer: a pilgrim

palsied: suffering from a disease of the nervous system leading either to paralysis or involuntary muscular movement

pate: the head or the skull

penn: a pen, a small enclosure for farm animals

perfidy: betrayal of trust or breach of faith

plaint: a complaint or lamentation

plevir: the plover (bird)

ply: to employ or to work busily at

pole-cat: a small, dark-brown carnivorous quadruped of the weasel family

proffer: to offer or propose

ptarmigan: a member of the grouse family which inhabits high altitudes in Scotland

rack: clouds or driving mist or fog

raike: to range over, to wander through

raile: a bodice; the upper portion of an infant's night dress

rankling: festering or embittering

reave: see note on 44, l. 400

red-beam: a reflection of the sunset

reel: a lively dance

reign: realm

reile: the spool of a spinning wheel, a bobbin (reel)

remede: redress, remedy

reuth: compassion, pity

rill: a small stream or brook

riven: cracked, fissured, or split

roe: a small species of deer

rok: a distaff with wool or flax attached; the quantity of wool or flax placed on the distaff for spinning (*rock*)

ronkled: gnarled (see *SND* under *runkle*)

rood: a cross

roundelay: short song with refrain

rout: see note on 15, l. 5

rowar: a roll of newly-carded wool ready to be spun (see *SND*

under *row* v.[1], n., I. 19. (5) (iv))
rowe: to roll
rueful: exciting sorrow or compassion; lamentable; dismal

sable: black; a symbol of mourning or grief
sae: so
sair: bitterly
scan: to examine, interpret, or assign meaning to
scathe: to harm, to injure; harm or injury
schaw: a grove, a thicket
screen: to hold from view, to shield
se: the sea
sear: to wither, to scorch
sea-rack: clouds or fog coming in from the sea
sear'd: withered or blighted
sen: since
servitor: a male personal or domestic servant
shieling: a hut of rough construction erected near a pasture in which cattle graze
shill: shrill
shrive: to hear confession
signet: a private seal for use as authentication
sikn: such
siller: silver
sire: a father
slot: track of deer, as shown by footprints
snoode: a ribbon for tying hair
sorel: a buck in its third year
spak: spoke
speile: to climb, to clamber up
sponsal'd: married or wedded
staid: i.e. 'stayed', in the sense of 'checked', 'stopped'
starveling: deprived of food
staw: stole
steile: a needle
strain: a stream or flow of impassioned language
strath: a wide valley, normally

transversed by a river and bounded by hills
strayne: a stream or flow of impassioned language
streamourie: flashing with streams of light, like the aurora borealis
sturt: trouble, disquiet
suborn: to induce by underhand or unlawful means a person to commit a misdeed; to corrupt
swain: a young rustic or a country labourer; a shepherd
swarth: dark
swaw: to glide
swoof: to make a rustling or whizzing sound, as of the wind, or a bird in flight

thriven: flourished or prospered
tiar: a tiara or ornamental head-dress
til: to
tod: the fox
trace: the track left by a person or animal in walking or running
traissel: a track left by footsteps
troth: pledge of marriage
trow: to believe
tyrling: swirling (from *tirl*)

unbrookable: intolerable
unhousell'd: see note on 55, l. 161
unstaid: unsteady or unstable
unweeting: unwitting or unknowing

vele: a stringed musical instrument, a viol
vesper: an evening song; the sixth of the canonical hours of prayer
viands: food

wa: a wall
wae: woe; sorrowful
waesome, waesum: woesome
waly: an exclamation of sorrow
wanyirdlye: unearthly
ward: one who is under the control or protection of a guardian

waring: avoiding
warrant: protection, authorisation
warre: to employ (from *ware*)
weal: welfare or well-being
weel: well
ween: to think or to surmise
weetless: unknowing, unconscious
weir: war, warfare
welkin: the sky, the firmament
wha: who
whelpish: youthful or puppy-like
whet: to sharpen or put an edge on
wight: a human being
wilder'd: pathless, straying, or wandering
wimple: to meander, to ripple (of a stream)
winsomest: most pleasant
wist: knew; known (past tense and past participle of *wit,* to know)
wonit: dwelt
woo: wool
writhing: distorting
wroth: stirred to wrath, made angry

yean: of a ewe: to give birth to a lamb
yew: the yew tree, often planted in churchyards, is used in poetry as a symbol of sadness or death
yirde, yirthe: the earth
youl: to howl; to cry loudly or piteously
younker: a youngster

zenith: the highest point of the sky directly overhead as viewed from any particular position

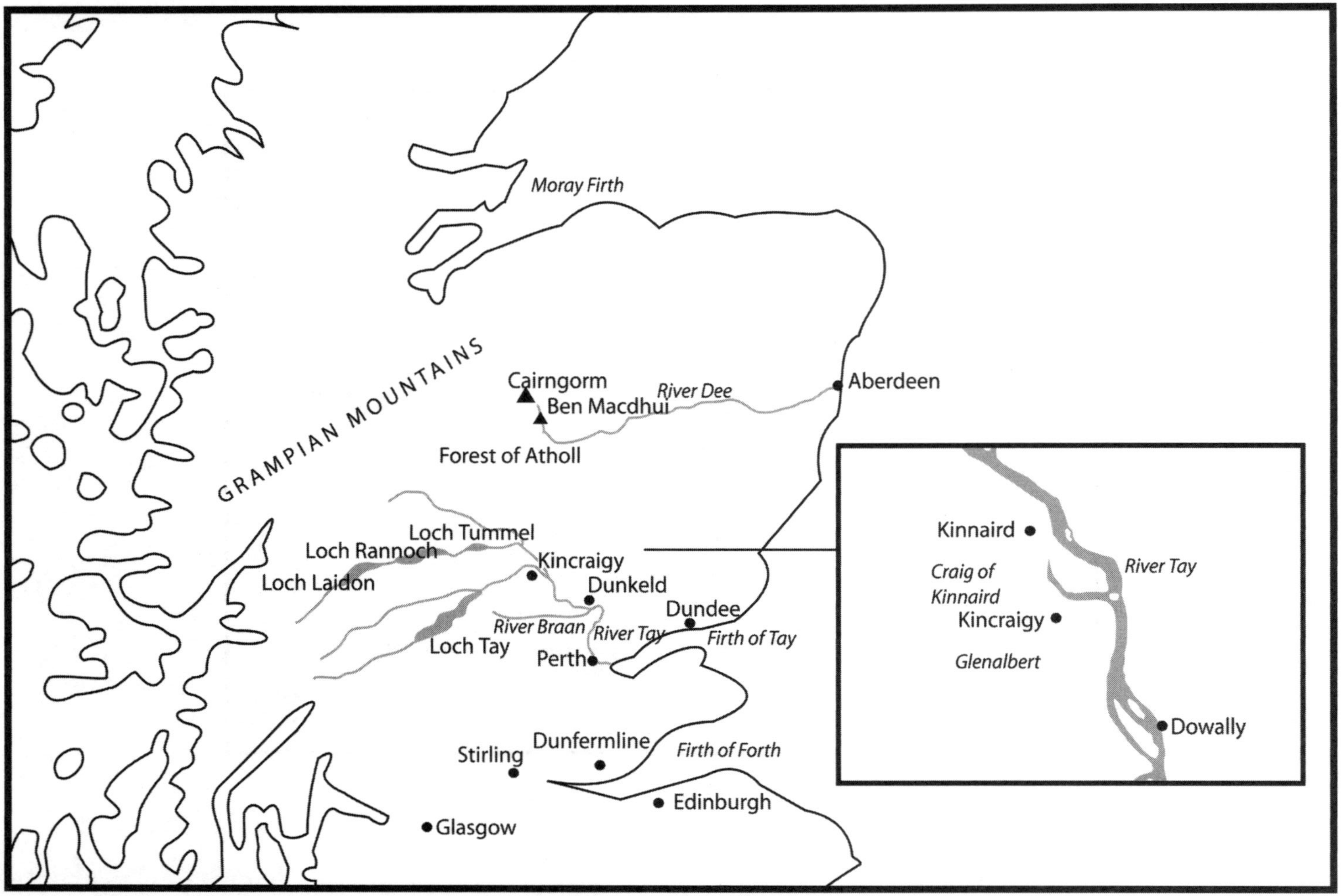

The River Tay and its Major Tributaries

Inset map labels:
Kinnaird
Craig of Kinnaird
Kincraigy
Glenalbert
Dowally
River Tay

Main map labels:
Moray Firth
River Dee
Cairngorm
Ben Macdhui
Forest of Atholl
GRAMPIAN MOUNTAINS
Aberdeen
Loch Tummel
Loch Rannoch
Loch Laidon
Kincraigy
Dunkeld
River Braan
Loch Tay
River Tay
Perth
Dundee
Firth of Tay
Firth of Forth
Stirling
Dunfermline
Edinburgh
Glasgow

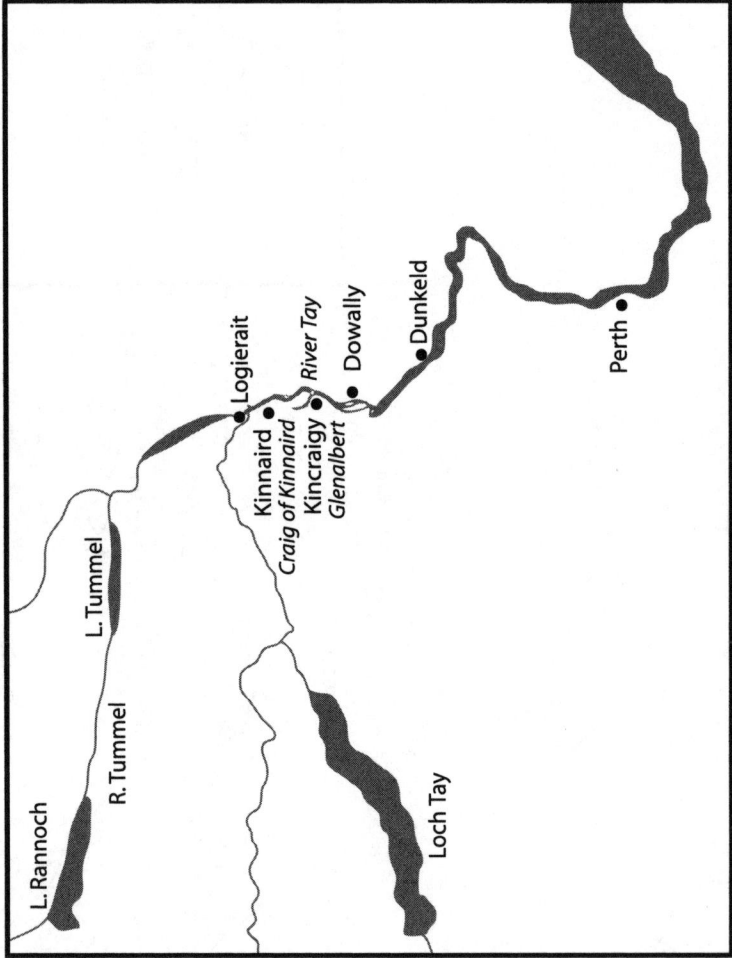

Kinnaird and Kincraigy

**FRANCIS CLOSE HALL
LEARNING CENTRE**
Swindon Road Cheltenham
Gloucestershire GL50 4AZ
Telephone: 01242 532913

UNIVERSITY OF
GLOUCESTERSHIRE
at CHELTENHAM *and* GLOUCESTER

NORMAL LOAN

44706 03/05